Wrestling with Words

The Five Parts of a Powerful Vocabulary Program

Aaron Daffern

Library of Congress Control Number: 2018909410

Copyright © 2018 David Aaron Daffern

All rights reserved. This book or any portion thereof may not be reproduced or used in any manner whatsoever without the express written permission of the author except for the use of brief quotations in a book review or scholarly journal.

First Printing: 2018

ISBN-13: 978-0-9990241-4-0

Aaron Daffern Consulting

www.AaronDaffern.com

Dedication

To every teacher who optimistically put up a vocabulary wall in August and never touched it again until May.

There is a better way.

Contents

	Acknowledgments	i
1	The Power of Words	3
2	Preparing for Vocabulary Instruction	13
3	Presenting New Words	23
4	Placing Words in Context	33
5	Basic Processing Tasks (Mastery/Understanding)	45
6	Basic Processing Tasks (Interpersonal/Self-Expressive)	59
7	Complex Processing Tasks	69
8	Playing with Words	81
9	Putting the Parts Together	93
	Appendix 1: Vocabulary Selection	99
	Appendix 2: Direct Vocabulary Instruction	109
	Appendix 3: Memory and Motivation	117
	References	129

Acknowledgements

I would like to thank Andrena for her work in proofreading this book and serving as a sounding board. Thank you for lending me your wisdom.

Chapter 1: The Power of Words

For too long vocabulary instruction has suffered as the annoying cousin at the family reunion of education. Some tolerate it, some disdain it, and still others only give it a perfunctory nod of acknowledgement. Greeted with awkward salutations, it quickly gets directed to the instructional children's table. Rather than well-researched teaching techniques, it normally consists of copying definitions or memorizing random lists of words for college readiness exams.

No more.

Vocabulary is power. Word knowledge translates directly to reading comprehension and literacy is the foundation of any education system. Instruction in word meaning should be viewed as much more than simply learning the definitions of highlighted terms in a textbook. First and foremost, vocabulary instruction has a significant effect on the comprehension of reading passages that contain the studied words. The amount of time spent on word study also has a strong correlation with passage comprehension. Additionally, residual effects come into play after quality vocabulary instruction. A smaller but still significant increase in comprehension exists for texts that do not include any of the studied words (Stahl & Fairbanks, 1986).

Vocabulary is one of the most important predictors of reading comprehension. It's a measure of verbal ability that serves as the foundation of all learning. It affects the reader's ability to make inferences critical to reading comprehension and to learn even more words (Blachowicz, Fisher, Ogle, & Watts-Taffe, 2006). The importance of word power begins at a very early age. Vocabulary knowledge in kindergarten and first grade is a significant predictor of reading comprehension in the middle and secondary grades (Brief, 2008).

Insight into vocabulary terms relates strongly with reading comprehension (Beck & McKeown, 1991; Brief, 2008; Mebarki, 2011; Nagy, 1988; Nagy & Herman, 1984; Nagy & Townsend, 2012; Smith, 1997). In a meta-analysis of the effects of hundreds of teaching techniques that affect learning, vocabulary instruction was found to have an effect size of 0.67, well within the range of strategies that impact achievement above and beyond basic instruction (Fisher, Frey, & Hattie, 2016). More than test scores are at stake, however. Vocabulary knowledge affects a student's ability to participate fully in social and academic classroom routines (Blachowicz, Fisher, & Watts-Taffe, 2005).

Incidental Word Learning

While the majority of this book is dedicated to how to teach vocabulary words directly and have students meaningfully interact with them, another consideration must be kept in mind. Most children learn words at a phenomenal rate apart from any specific vocabulary instruction on the part of a teacher. In a typical classroom program, around 300 words are taught in a year (Nagy & Herman, 1984). Compare that, however, with the estimate that students typically learn anywhere from 2,000 to 4,000 words per year (Anderson & Nagy, 1993; Graves, 2016; Graves & Fitzgerald, 2006; Nagy, 1988; Nagy & Herman, 1984).

This means that about 90% of the words students learn each and every year come from incidental exposure while only roughly 10% come from intentional word study (Carlisle, 2007). This is not to say, though, that direct vocabulary instruction is relatively ineffective. While the majority of learned words come through secondary interactions, solid vocabulary instruction, which this book seeks to outline in detail, can in fact set into motion an accumulated advantage for well-taught students. Sometimes referred to as the Matthew Effect, this adage states that in certain conditions the rich get richer and the poor get poorer. Though only affecting the relatively small portion of learned terms, solid vocabulary instruction helps students learn all words more efficiently and effectively.

A Well-Rounded Program

Successful vocabulary instruction is something that is modeled, not assigned, by a teacher. Educators who love words develop students who love words. For vocabulary instruction to be effective, teachers must themselves be interested in learning new words. When it is seen as a quest for knowledge rather than a task for a grade, students approach word learning with energy and enthusiasm (Blachowicz & Fisher, 2011).

Before moving on to the various aspects of direct vocabulary instruction beginning in the second chapter, it would be wise to consider all the components of a successful vocabulary program. While the centerpiece is teacher-driven, other support pieces come into play to strengthen student interaction with vocabulary terms.

Many leading literacy experts agree that a well-rounded program consists of four major components. The first three will be examined briefly while the final section will be delved into deeply throughout the remainder of this book. Ideal word learning includes wide reading by students, teaching word learning strategies, fostering word consciousness, and direct instruction on the part of the teacher (Blachowicz, Fisher, Ogle, & Watts-Taffe, 2006; Graves, 2015/2016; Graves & Fitzgerald, 2006; Mebarki, 2011; Phillips, Foote, & Harper, 2008; Scott & Nagy, 2009).

Wide Reading

Remember that this book deals with only 10% of vocabulary growth. Most new words are learned incidentally and teachers can do much to encourage wide reading among students. Not only does it increase unscripted vocabulary knowledge, it is an effective method of acquiring new information. The more students read, the more general knowledge they accumulate. This will, in turn, improve reading comprehension (Nagy & Herman, 1984). The purpose of vocabulary instruction is to increase knowledge and literacy, both of which work hand-in-hand with reading.

Promoting wide reading also helps learners adapt to various literary forms. Teachers naturally aim to include texts in multiple genres and media forms to lure students into literacy. When students have ready access to drama, fables, fairy tales, historical fiction, poetry, and fantasy/science fiction, they grow adept at interpreting fictional modalities. On the other hand, there is much information to be found in biographies/autobiographies, essays, narrative nonfiction, and traditional textbooks. Add to that blog posts, graphic novels, wikis, podcasts, and a horde of emerging digital media, and students will never claim they have nothing to read.

With wide reading focusing more on exposure and general interest than specific reading instruction, teachers might consider grouping books by genre rather than by reading level. Students interested in science fiction will naturally be drawn to similar books if they have ready access to them, regardless of their difficulty. Purposeful visits to the school library can expose students to a variety of genres and increase their interest in reading. Additionally, teachers can send home book recommendations for students to check out from a local library.

As the term implies, wide reading is more about breadth than depth. While normal classroom instruction naturally includes deep reading with specific text objectives, wide reading is more about exposure. By building an instructional environment that is rich and varied, life-long learning is reinforced (Graves & Fitzgerald, 2006). The texts themselves should be sufficiently worthwhile with mature vocabulary rather than watered-down and simplified (Pressley, Disney, & Anderson, 2007). Since a substantial amount of vocabulary growth comes from reading rather than direct instruction, language-rich environments do much to foster word awareness (Anderson & Nagy, 1993; Phillips, Foote, & Harper, 2008).

The remainder of this book notwithstanding, the best way to build a child's vocabulary is to promote wide reading. Time spent reading a variety of texts will lead to gains in fluency, prior knowledge, familiarity with many different written forms, and an appreciation of multiple genres (Anderson & Nagy, 1993). Increasing the volume and variety of student's reading an essential part of promoting large-scale vocabulary growth (Fisher, Frey, & Hattie, 2016; Nagy, 1988).

Word Learning Strategies

If simple exposure were enough, vocabulary instruction would be as easy as assigning reading time during school hours. To make the most of wide reading, however, students need to be armed with word learning strategies. As they develop as independent word learners, students greatly increase their rate of vocabulary growth as they encounter new words (Graves & Fitzgerald, 2006; Scott & Nagy, 2009).

Several techniques exist that can help learners self-monitor as they interact with unknown terms. Rather than being examined separately, however, these strategies will be discussed in detail in later sections of this book. Teachers should model good word learning behaviors for students, showing them that careful thought and intentionality are key components for understanding and remembering new words (Phillips, Foote, & Harper, 2008). Some examples are the use of mnemonics or keywords (chapter 5) and various kinds of graphic organizers (chapter 4).

Another way that students can become conscious word detectives is to be on the lookout for generative elements, such as prefixes, suffixes, or base words (Blachowicz, Fisher, Ogle, & Watts-Taffe, 2006; Carlisle, 2007). While learning one base word, many related terms can be easily derived. This shows the connectivity of language and is examined more closely as part of the ABCs of direct vocabulary instruction (chapter 3).

Finally, students can oftentimes come to an approximate understanding of term by examining the surrounding passage for context clues (Carlisle, 2007; Graves, 2015/2016). Though not every passage is bristling with suggestions to help decipher unknown words, students should get in the habit of examining the surrounding sentences for possible hints. This mainstay of deciphering is also part of the ABCs of direct vocabulary instruction (chapter 3).

Word Consciousness

Both wide reading and word learning strategies help students develop a broader sense of word consciousness. This attitude can be described as an overall awareness of words and their meanings, how meanings change and grow, and a motivation to increase word knowledge (Blachowicz, Fisher, Ogle, & Watts-Taffe, 2006). It is supported by teachers who love words and show an interest in the power of vocabulary (Blachowicz & Fisher, 2011). Word consciousness feeds on word-rich environments that have a variety of literacy materials with both motivational and instructional value (Blachowicz & Fisher, 2004a; Blachowicz, Fisher, Ogle, & Watts-Taffe, 2006).

Word consciousness transcends mere vocabulary. More than simply a fun activity or an effective teaching technique, word consiousness is a frame of mind. It involves thinking metacognitively about word choice and why certain terms work better than others. This heightened sensitivity translates to a cognizance of encounters with new words and improves vocabulary acquisition (Blachowicz, Fisher, & Watts-Taffe, 2005; Graves & Fitzgerald, 2006; Scott & Nagy, 2009).

Teachers can influence word consciousness in a variety of ways. First, they should put an emphasis on word use during everyday classroom discussions and lessons. Students should see that word choice and selection are important at all times, not just during scripted vocabulary lessons. As they read, write, listen, and discuss different topics at school, the words they select are an important component of linguistic expression (Scott & Nagy, 2009).

Teachers can add to this by being on the lookout for interesting phrases and terms. As a teacher, discuss why you like a certain wording and its effect on meaning. This will provide a metacognitive link between an author's word choice and the response of the reader. It's not only what words are used but how they are interpreted that contribute to the overall understanding of a passage (Scott & Nagy, 2009).

Additionally, teachers can challenge students to formulate hypotheses about the meaning of challenging or complex terms. Rather than quickly abridging the cognitive struggle of students, teachers can ask students to use word parts, prior knowledge, and/or context clues to help build a possible definition. When appropriate, students should also take care to note any nuance of meaning and be sensitive to various connotations. This helps develop a curiosity about word meanings and heightens word analysis skills (Anderson & Nagy, 1993).

Direct Instruction

The fourth component of a well-rounded program is what most think of when considering vocabulary instruction. How teachers approach word learning and the type of activities they plan for students goes a long way toward supporting vocabulary acquisition. While it may seem like a fairly simple task on the surface, there are several layers of complexity that separate superior instruction from memorizing static definitions.

The first component to be considered is which words are worthy of attention. Chapter 2 looks at the various components of preparing for vocabulary instruction. Teachers should first evaluate potential terms in light of their importance to the text and usefulness beyond the immediate context. As words increase in one or both areas, their value also rises. Another aspect to consider is student evaluation of potential words. Student motivation and buy-in will improve if they have a voice in which words to study. A more technical review of proper vocabulary selection can be found in appendix 1.

Once potential words have been culled, teachers should make the most of how they present the terms to students. Specifically, seven powerful components are looked at in chapter 3. When teachers share a word's meaning, they should activate prior knowledge and examine any word parts such as bases or affixes. If context clues can help understand the word, those should be explored along with a descriptive definition. Examples and non-examples, synonyms, and even grammar usage can also help students learn new words. The multitude of research supporting these components is pored over in appendix 2.

After teachers have introduced the words to the students, the burden of work shifts. Students should first work to place the words in context so they relate them to what is already known (chapter 4). Additionally, various types of processing tasks (chapters 5-7) help students wrestle with the words and build a more robust understanding. Finally, word learning can be immensely enjoyable. Playing with words (chapter 8) is another important component that builds flexibility and nimbleness in word usage.

Underlying all of these strategies and activities are two major structures spelled out in appendix 3. First, how students construct knowledge is of vital importance to all learning, not simply vocabulary instruction. Students need to actively construct knowledge, not passively receive it. When new learning is tied to known content through multiple pathways, recall is improved. Additionally, cementing new information into long-term memory requires repeated exposures over time.

Second, students are motivated to learn by five major facets: competence, relationships, autonomy, value, and emotions. When instructional design meets student motivation, classroom engagement is bolstered. The teaching techniques, methods, and activities presented in this book are built on the truths of memory and motivation.

Put simply, wrestling with words is an essential component of any instructional program. The central pier of education is literacy and the core of literacy is word knowledge. Yet how often is it given the priority it deserves? Keep reading and discover the five parts of a powerful vocabulary program.

CHAPTER 2: PREPARING FOR VOCABULARY INSTRUCTION

All words are not created equal. In the limited amount of time that teachers have for vocabulary instruction, several factors must be considered before proceeding. Instead of simply teaching any words that happen to be highlighted in yellow by the textbook publisher, teachers should first examine the selection itself. If a word appears frequently but its meaning can be resolved using analysis of surrounding context or word structure (e.g., roots, affixes), the word is not a good candidate for direct instruction. Likewise, if the term appears often enough that its repetition will greatly assist in understanding its meaning, the focus should be on different words (Fisher, Frey, & Hattie, 2016).

When deciding upon words that require direct instruction, the selection process itself should be considered. Will the teacher choose the words or will the students? Another option is to blend the two and allow students some choice while retaining a set of words that all students will examine. Those words that are both *useful* and *important* and cannot be learned by other means should be the ones taught to students (Kelley, Lesaux, Kieffer, & Faller, 2010). For a more complete examination of the word selection process, please see appendix 1.

Teacher Choice

Words that are useful have value beyond the text or unit of study. Rather than having limited use, these words will most likely be seen in other selections or even across various subjects. Learning useful words looks past the lesson at hand and contributes to the overall vocabulary knowledge of students.

Another criteria by which words should be judged is their importance to the text itself. As helpful as it is to study words that add to general language development, the text or current topic of study must first be understood. Sometimes there are key words upon which comprehension hinges and it is these essential terms that demand attention. Without a firm understanding of their meaning, the gist of the passage might not be grasped by students.

Teachers can and should use their judgment when deciding upon the usefulness and importance of various words. One method which can be used to aid in the selection process is a technique called 4-Quadrant Vocabulary.

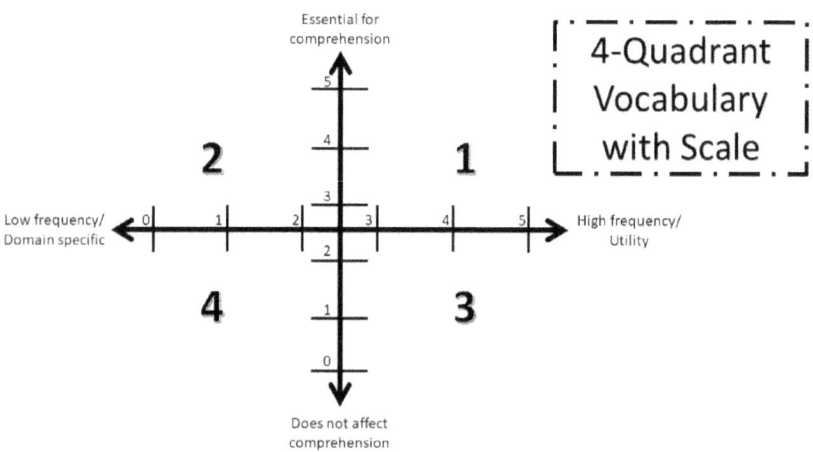

Figure 1: 4-Quadrant Vocabulary with Scale

Similar to a coordinate plane in mathematics, words can be graphed by measuring their usefulness outside of the text (horizontal axis) and their importance to the text (vertical axis). However, the four quadrants are labeled in a different manner than those use in traditional graphing. The best words for inclusion are those that rate high in both usefulness and importance (first quadrant).

If both of those conditions are not met, however, and lesser words must be included, it is those words which rank high in importance that should win out (second quadrant). Since the words are to be studied in the context of a text selection or larger unit, understanding that passage is essential. The third option would be words that do not have high importance to the text but contribute to the general knowledge of the student (third quadrant). Finally, words in the fourth quadrant (low usefulness and importance) can most likely be ignored altogether.

Table 1: Questions for 4-Quadrant Vocabulary with Scale

Usefulness (horizontal axis)	Importance (vertical axis)
1. Are the students likely to encounter this word in other texts?	1. Is the word essential to the reading selection or unit of study?
2. Does the word relate to another topic in the classroom?	2. Will the reader not understand a major idea or concept without a good understanding of the word?
3. Is the word commonly used outside of the selection or theme?	3. Does the word play a role in communicating the meaning of the context in which it is used?
4. Is the word representative of a family of words important for learning in general?	4. Is the word or phrase representative of a concept the students will need to know?
5. Is this a word that will heighten students' enthusiasm for word learning?	5. Does the word bring clarity or specificity to the text or situation?

For those that prefer more structure in evaluating words based on these two criteria, a series of questions can be used to clarify the worth of each word (Table 1). For every positive answer to one of the questions, the word gains 1 point in either usefulness or importance. For example, if a word receives three affirmations from usefulness questions (horizontal axis) and four from importance questions (vertical axis), that would place it in the first quadrant. The 4-Quadrant Vocabulary graph is a quick, visual way to evaluate and select the words that will have the biggest impact on student learning.

Regarding the amount of words to be studied, this varies greatly based on the size of the selection or unit and the age-level of the students. When in doubt, however, the axiom "less is more" is a good rule to follow. Though studying ten or even twenty words is possible, typically limiting the study to four to seven words allows for a deeper examination by students.

In addition, the timing and intensity of the instruction should be considered once essential words have been chosen. Flanigan and Greenwood (2007) suggest sorting words into three levels of instruction. Level 1 words are critical "before" words that require an in-depth understanding before reading. These words should be taught intensely to provide students the tools necessary to successfully navigate the test.

Level 2 "foot-in-the-door" words are also important but not central to comprehending the main idea of the text. If these words represent familiar concepts with an unfamiliar label, they can be explained by providing a definition or synonym. If they represent an unfamiliar concept, typically giving a definition and using the term in a sentence will be sufficient.

Level 3 "after" words are those that can be taught during or after the reading of the selection. These words usually are either defined in the text or are surrounded by a rich context that provides clues to their meaning.

Taken together, teachers can use 4-Quadrant Vocabulary and the three-level framework to choose which words to teach and where they fit in the instructional cycle. By selecting words that have the most leverage in terms of usefulness and importance, instructional efficiency is promoted. By evaluating the prior knowledge of students and the structure of the text, teachers can decide whether the words need brief or intense pre-instruction or if the text itself can be used to define the words. The next chapter looks exclusively at the various methods teachers can use to teach vocabulary words.

Student Choice

Any time that students have the ability to make choices in their learning, their sense of ownership and autonomy rises dramatically. Rather than being handed a list of words that they might not identify with, involving students in the decision-making process is a great way to motivate and engage them (Blachowicz, Fisher, Ogle, & Watts-Taffe, 2006; Phillips, Foote, & Harper, 2008).

Instead of a free-for-all, however, in which teachers are worried that students will choose the easiest words possible to study, students should take a moment to rank words based on their own level of word knowledge. This provides not only motivation for students but allows for more personalized learning.

After teachers have selected a pool of potential words to study using 4-Quadrant Vocabulary, they can share the word bank with students. Students can quickly read the list and give each word a rank from one to four. Words they've never heard (or read) before should receive a one. Words they are generally familiar with but aren't quite sure about receive a two.

If students know what a word means and feel they can give a simple definition or synonym, they should give it a rank of three. Finally, words they are comfortable using in self-generated speaking or writing should receive a four. This last rank is reserved for words they can use in a variety of contexts and situations.

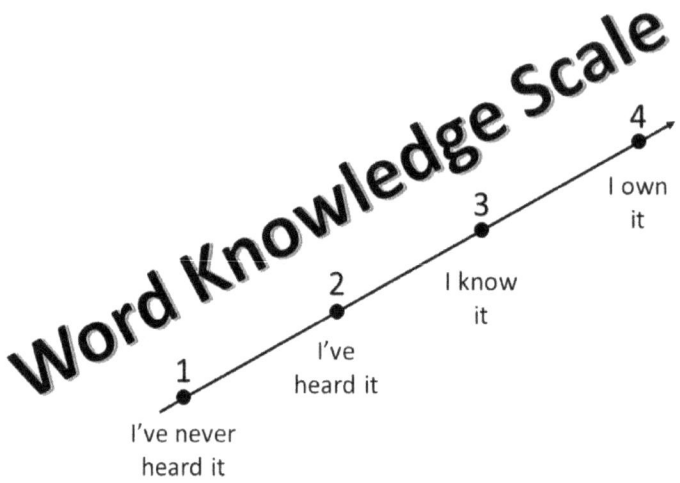

Figure 2: Word Knowledge Scale

After each student has ranked the word bank, they can choose a set of words for their personal study throughout the unit. They should select words that are ranked either one, two, or three. Since rank four words are already known to them, they should be excluded from direct vocabulary study.

It is at this point that teachers can decide whether to allow students to select all words for study or to mandate a few words that will be studied as a class. For example, a teacher might want students to study six to eight words while working with a particular selection. She might have four words that are first quadrant words and want all students to work with them. She could include six other words from the second and third quadrants and ask students to rate them using the Word Knowledge Scale. Finally, she can ask them to choose two to four words that are either rank one, two, or three to include with the four words she's already chosen.

Giving students the ability to choose words they'd like to study motivates them by activating the facet of autonomy. In addition, having students rate their level of word knowledge also motivates them through the facet of value (read more about autonomy and value in appendix 3). When student are asked to think metacognitively and reflect on their own experiences, it communicates respect to them. They have the opportunity to work with words that potentially have more relevancy to their interests. This will increase their engagement and attention to detail.

Using the Word Knowledge Scale also gives students a chance to build their confidence in their language usage. After assigning each word a rank and instruction has been completed, students can rank each word again as a post-assessment. The difference between the first and second rankings will represent their vocabulary growth. They can even graph the results with a bar or line graph to visually see their level of competence grow.

Vignette

Mr. Wilson examined Hans Christian Anderson's *The Ugly Duckling* and thought about its message. He wanted to study it next week with his 4th grade students but thought that some of the terms might be too advanced for them. Nevertheless, he reread the story and decided that it would be a great opportunity to hold a larger discussion about societal expectations and fitting in.

He wanted to spend most of his time with the climax of the fairy tale. Looking at the final few paragraphs, he underlined several words that he thought might be unfamiliar to his students.

"Kill me," said the poor bird; and he bent his head down to the surface of the water, and awaited death.

But what did he see in the clear stream below? His own image; no longer a dark, gray bird, ugly and <u>disagreeable</u> to look at, but a <u>graceful</u> and beautiful swan. To be born in a duck's nest, in a farmyard, is of <u>no consequence</u> to a bird, if it is hatched from a swan's egg. He now felt glad at having suffered <u>sorrow</u> and trouble, because it enabled him to enjoy so much better all the pleasure and happiness around him; for the great swans swam round the <u>new-comer</u>, and <u>stroked</u> his neck with their *beaks, as a welcome.*

Into the garden presently came some little children, and threw bread and cake into the water.

"See," cried the youngest, "there is a new one;" and the rest were delighted, and ran to their father and mother, dancing and clapping their hands, and shouting <u>joyously</u>, "There is another swan come; a new one has arrived."

Then they threw more bread and cake into the water, and said, "The new one is the most beautiful of all; he is so young and pretty." And the old swans bowed their heads before him.

Then he felt quite <u>ashamed</u>, and hid his head under his wing; for he did not know what to do, he was so happy, and yet not at all proud. He had been <u>persecuted</u> and <u>despised</u> for his ugliness, and now he heard them say he was the most beautiful of all the birds. Even the <u>elder-tree</u> bent down its bows into the water before him, and the sun shone warm and bright. Then he <u>rustled</u> his feathers, curved his <u>slender</u> neck, and cried <u>joyfully</u>, from the depths of his heart, "I never dreamed of such happiness as this, while I was an ugly duckling." (Anderson, 1872)

After reviewing his markups, he realized he had underlined 14 words or phrases. He knew this was far too many words to study so he used 4-Quadrant Vocabulary to identify which words he wanted to focus on. Using the five questions to evaluate how useful and important each word or phrase was, he came up with the following designations:

First quadrant: *ashamed, persecuted, sorrow*

Second quadrant: *disagreeable, despised, graceful*

Third quadrant: *joyfully, joyously, rustled, slender, stroked*

Fourth quadrant: *no consequence, newcomer, elder-tree*

Since *ashamed*, *persecuted*, and *sorrow* had the most usefulness and were important to know for general comprehension, he wanted to highlight those three words through direct instruction. The fourth quadrant words (*no consequence*, *newcomer*, and *elder-tree*) could be skipped without affecting the meaning of the text.

That only left the second and third quadrant words. Of those, he wanted to ask the students to use context clues to help them define *joyously* (e.g., *delighted*, *dancing*, *clapping their hands*). He hoped they could use the similarities between the roots of *joyously* and *joyfully* to help define the latter.

The remaining second and third quadrant words (i.e., *disagreeable*, *despised*, *graceful*, *rustled*, *slender*, *stroked*) may or may not already be known to a certain degree by his students. Instead of overloading his students with vocabulary words, he wanted to present them with options. He asked them to rank each of those remaining words using the Word Knowledge Scale.

"Students, we are going to read a very famous fairy tale called *The Ugly Duckling*. As always, there are going to be some vocabulary words to study. Please write down these three words in your vocabulary journals for us to look at later: *ashamed*, *persecuted*, *sorrow*.

"There are more unfamiliar words than those but I'd like to see how much you already know about them. I'm going to pass out a list to each of you and I want you to put a number from one to four next to each word." Mr. Wilson passed each student a paper with the following words: *disagreeable*, *despised*, *graceful*, *rustled*, *slender*, *stroked*.

He continued, "As you read each word, think about how much you know about it. Take a look at this scale I'm putting on the screen. Rank one words are those you've never heard of before. Put a one next to any word on the list that is unfamiliar to you.

"Rank two words are those you've heard of but you're not 100% sure you can tell me what they mean. If you put a three next to a word, that means you definitely know what it means. Finally, rank four is the rarest of all. If you own a word, that means you've read it many times and know how it's used in many different areas. You also can use the word in your own conversations without wondering if you've used it correctly."

The students quickly poured over the words and wrote a one, two, three, or four next to each one. When they had finished ranking the words, he concluded his instructions. "I want you to choose three or four words from this list that you'd like to study in addition to the three I've already had you write down. If you ranked any words as a four, that means you already own that word and it wouldn't do much good to study it anymore."

As he expected, someone raised his hand and asked, "Can we do more than four words?"

He smiled as he responded, "Yes, you can study more than four if you'd like but I'm only requiring three or four. It's your choice so choose the words you'd like to know more about." His students were bursting with anticipation to begin reading *The Ugly Duckling* and learn more about the words they chose. He knew that his students would not only improve their understanding of the fairy tale through focused word study, their general knowledge would also increase.

Chapter 3: Presenting New Words

Vocabulary instruction is not about teaching new words. If that were the case, the use of a dictionary and/or a thesaurus would be sufficient. Instead, vocabulary instruction is about teaching concepts. Instead of impotent definitions that are useless outside of a textbook, teachers should aim to share knowledge through the vehicle of vocabulary (Nagy, 1988).

The ultimate goal of vocabulary instruction is that students will learn how words represent an idea or concept. New knowledge needs to be incorporated into what is already known by the students. This is accomplished when multiple teaching strategies are employed to build a rich framework of understanding for the target words. For a more complete examination of the research supporting direct vocabulary instruction, please see appendix 2.

The ABCs of Direct Vocabulary Instruction

To fully develop a student's understanding of a new word, the concept must be presented in a variety of ways. It does a student no good to memorize a static definition and then be unable to apply that knowledge when the word is used in a slightly different way. To move toward a rank four understanding of words, to help students *own* them, there are seven different methods that research has shown to be instructionally sound.

Teachers can view these seven techniques as a menu to choose from in order to keep instruction from becoming routine and monotonous. If words are presented through multiple avenues, perhaps even four or five from the list, instructional effectiveness will skyrocket.

The ABCs of Vocabulary Instruction
Activate prior knowledge
Bases/affixes
Context clues
Descriptive definition
Examples/non-examples
Friendly words/synonyms
Grammar usage

Figure 3: ABCs of Direct Vocabulary Instruction

Activate Prior Knowledge

Remembering that the goal of vocabulary instruction is to increase general knowledge, helping students access what they already know about a concept is vital. This helps students associate the term with existing knowledge and greatly increases recall. Rather than starting the discussion with the new word as the object, teachers can generally speak about the concept without mentioning the word itself. Once students have begun to get a picture of the new idea, the word can be presented to give students a label for a concept they are beginning to explore (Nagy, 1988).

For example, if social studies students were learning the word *antebellum*, it would be very appropriate to begin with a conversation about how the word fits into what they have already been learning.

"We've been studying the U.S. Civil War for a few days now. We know that this event in the 19th century was one of the watershed events in our nation's history. It marks a division in our country's timeline, especially as it concerns the culture and heritage of the South. Before the war, slavery, large plantations, and gallant chivalry dominated Southern culture. Afterwards, the devastation of the war, the Emancipation Proclamation, and Reconstruction politics forever changed the lives of Southerners.

"When we discuss U.S. history in the South, it's very important to note whether the topic we are talking about took place before or after the war. There is a term that we can use to quickly note if something took place before the Civil War. One vocabulary word we will be looking at this week is *antebellum*. Even though it can be used to describe something that happened before any war, it usually refers to Southern life before the U.S. Civil War."

By first activating the prior study of American history, the students in the example have a ready network of information in which to place the new word. It is much easier for students to learn new labels for existing knowledge than new labels for unknown content (Nagy & Herman, 1984).

Activating prior knowledge also increases the desire to learn new terms by making the information valuable and meaningful. When students have a need or desire to succinctly express an idea or thought, they are much more likely to remember a vocabulary word that does just that (Nagy & Herman, 1984). Memory is greatly aided when new information relates to something that is already known (Willis, 2006).

Bases/Affixes

Effective vocabulary instruction provides many types of information about each word. This multi-faceted approach creates a more complete picture of what words mean and allows for better recall and transfer of new terms. One aspect of teaching words that also supports word analysis skills is the use of bases or affixes (Blachowicz, Fisher, Ogle, & Watts-Taffe, 2006).

When examining vocabulary for various word parts, a few questions can be asked. Are there any prefixes or suffixes that help add meaning to the word? Is there a root word within the term that can be used to explore other related words? How will knowledge of these word parts help students analyze other related words?

"If you look at the word *antebellum*, you'll notice that it has a prefix *ante-*. That's a good term to know because it means 'before' like the prefix 'pre-.'

"Another word with the same prefix is *antechamber*. Taking what you know of *ante-*, you can guess that an *antechamber* is something before a room. In fact, an *antechamber* is a small room that serves as a gateway into a larger room or reception area.

"Finally, if you've ever played a game of poker, you know that before you play each round some or all of the players have to put a small amount of chips into the pot. This is called the *ante* because it happens before anyone sees their cards."

Context Clues

Sometimes there is sufficient support from the surrounding text to aid readers in identifying unknown words. Since the vast majority of unknown words are learned through wide reading rather than direct instruction, strengthening word learning strategies is vital. These words provide a golden opportunity to help students use analysis and problem solving skills to improve their comprehension.

When appropriate, discussing words in a rich context is more effective and natural than simply providing them with definitions (Blachowicz, Fisher, & Watts-Taffe, 2005). This further reinforces the fact that words derive much of their meanings from their surroundings.

Sometimes words take on different connotations based on how they are used.

"Let's examine the sentence in the book that has one of our vocabulary words. 'The *antebellum* era is often associated with slavery, conflict, and sprawling Southern plantations.' There are several clues in the sentence that could help us define the word *antebellum* even if we hadn't already discussed it.

"First we see that *antebellum* is used as an adjective to describe era. This lets us know that *antebellum* refers to a specific time period in our history. The fact that it is often associated with slavery lets me know that the era happened before slavery was abolished after the Civil War.

"When it says that the *antebellum* era is also associated with conflict, that also makes me think that the Civil War is involved since that is the largest conflict in our history that involved slavery. Finally, Southern plantations being associated with the *antebellum* era lets us determine the geographic location associated with the word *antebellum* – the Southern states."

Not all contexts provide ample clues to help define a word. Rather than stretching the plausibility of the evidence, look for natural clues that might exist. Don't spend so much time trying to link a clue to a vocabulary word that the focus of the exercise is lost.

Descriptive Definition

As expected, a large part of vocabulary instruction revolves around defining unknown terms. How the definition is crafted, though, can do much to help or hinder understanding. Sometimes definitions from the dictionary or glossary include unknown terms and muddy rather than clear up the word's meaning.

Since words are used to define other words, a key to remember is that the definition needs to be in language that is easy to understand. The purpose is to convey meaning and that requires that the words used to define the unknown term are themselves understood. Instead of a tightly-controlled definition that is sparse and technical, definitions should be given in a more conversational style first before the technical definition is explored (Marzano & Pickering, 2005).

> "*Antebellum* is a descriptive term that places something or someone in a particular period in history. Most of the time it's used, it refers to something that happened before the American Civil War. Though it can be used to describe something that happened before any war, it typically is reserved for this particular conflict.
>
> "What's more, over the years it has been mostly used to refer to something in the Southern states before the Civil War. Even though Northern, Western, and Southern states had unique cultures, architecture, and customs before the Civil War, *antebellum*, which literally means "before the war," usually refers to Southern society before 1861."

By describing the term in everyday language and providing a thorough explanation, it helps builds knowledge in a more natural way (Beck, McKeown, Wagner, Muse, & Tannenbaum, 2007). As students encounter learned words in new contexts, they have a much deeper conceptual framework to use when applying new-found definitions.

Examples/Non-examples

One of the best ways to reinforce new vocabulary words is to compare and contrast them to known concepts (Graves & Fitzgerald, 2006). For some students, a definition or contextual support might not be enough to understand a word. Instead, they need to see how the new term plays out when it interacts with their prior knowledge.

> "Let's look at a few examples of *antebellum* to see how it's used. This picture of a plantation house from Georgia, built in the

1820s, can be described as an *antebellum* plantation because it's typical of Southern architecture before the Civil War.

"This picture of a dress can also be described as an *antebellum* dress because it was fashionable in the decade before the Civil War. More importantly, the style was seen a lot in balls and dances held in Southern states during that time, another requirement for use of the term *antebellum*.

"This picture of a New England shipyard could not be described as *antebellum*, however. Even though you see it is dated 1834, well before the Civil War, its location, the North, is not where our term *antebellum* usually refers to. If this shipyard happened to be in South Carolina or Virginia, then we could then call it *antebellum*."

Sometimes what is known about a word is strengthened as much by what it isn't as by what it is. Giving examples and non-examples of vocabulary words allows for the exploration of the nuances of terms. Understanding is refined by explaining why something is or isn't an example of the word under consideration.

Friendly Words/Synonyms

Another method that can be used to help give shape to words is to provide synonyms. Sometimes called "friendly words" in the primary grades, synonyms provide another method for students to tie something unknown (i.e., new vocabulary word) to something that is known (i.e., synonym). For words with clear-cut definitions that are familiar concepts with unfamiliar labels, sometimes a simple synonym is all that is needed for understanding (Graves, Baumann, & Blachowicz, 2014).

Friendly words also provide an opportunity to deepen the understanding of target terms. While they are synonyms, they invariably have different shades of meaning. These differences should be highlighted so that students can see how the words are similar but separate.

"Another way to think of the term *antebellum* is to remember the synonym *prewar*. We know that the prefix *pre-* means 'before' so if something is *prewar* that means it occurred before a war.

"One difference to keep in mind, however, is that *prewar* can be used as a general term. It doesn't refer to a particular war or geographic location. *Antebellum*, on the other hand, usually refers to the South before the Civil War."

As with context clues, not all words have reliable synonyms. If there are friendly words that can add texture to an unknown term, they should be explored. Be cautious, however. Straining the meaning of a word just to make it a synonym for a vocabulary term can be more confusing than helpful. Also, if the synonym itself is an unfamiliar term, it will not be very useful in learning a new word.

Grammar Usage

Finally, words should be placed in the proper context within language. Instead of standing alone as isolated terms, vocabulary words coexist and get meaning from their usage in written and spoken communication. Definitional, contextual, and usage information are all important pieces of successful vocabulary instruction (Blachowicz, Fisher, & Watts-Taffe, 2005).

Several factors should be considered when looking at how words are used in sentences. What part of speech is the word (e.g., noun, verb, adverb, etc.)? How does the word usage affect its meaning? Does the word have an origin that sheds light on its definition or use?

"One interesting thing about our term *antebellum* is that it is a direct translation from Latin. The word is made up of two Latin words – *ante*, which means 'before', and *bellum*, which means 'war.' Our word *antebellum* is literally the Latin phrase for 'before the war.'

"If you've ever heard of the word *bellicose* it's related to the

Latin word *bellum*. *Bellicose* means 'easily angered' or 'ready to fight' because it comes from the Latin word for war.

"In English, *antebellum* is used as an adjective. It describes things or events that happened before the Civil War. A plantation or a military uniform can be described as *antebellum*."

By highlighting the word's usage in English, students add another piece of knowledge about what the word means. Learning that a vocabulary word is an adjective, for example, communicates the fact that it is descriptive. Examining roots also provides an opportunity to extend learning beyond the vocabulary terms themselves and practice analysis skills (Pressley, Disney, & Anderson, 2007).

While these seven components all contribute to vocabulary acquisition, they should be viewed as a menu rather than as a set of directions. Highlighting each new word from all seven angles would be laborious. Use the ABCs of direct vocabulary instruction to choose a few different methods to introduce words in a variety of ways. Also consider the ages of the students. Younger students that have a vague or nonexistent understanding of grammar usage would get little benefit from knowing that a vocabulary word is an adverb.

Vignette

Mr. Wilson stopped the class after they had read the first sentence of the final paragraph of the story. He wanted to make sure that students really understood one of the words he had chosen as a first quadrant word – *ashamed*.

Then he felt quite <u>ashamed</u>, and hid his head under his wing; for he did not know what to do, he was so happy, and yet not at all proud.

"Let's pause a moment before we continue reading. Have any of you ever had an experience when you were a small child and you didn't know what to do? Maybe you felt confused or even sad because you were shy or unsure of yourself? If so, you know how the ugly duckling felt. It says that he felt quite ashamed and the word ashamed means to feel embarrassed.

"There is something that the ugly duckling does in this sentence that can help us with our vocabulary word. It says that he hid his head under his wing and that helps us understand that ashamed means to feel embarrassed. Sometimes when I feel ashamed I want to hide so no one can see me. The sentence also says that he didn't know what to do which can sometimes happen when you feel ashamed.

"I would feel ashamed if I spilled my lunch tray on my shirt in the cafeteria. Everyone would be looking at me and my clothes would be a mess. I wouldn't be ashamed if I was in a dark forest at night. Instead, I would be very scared, which is different from feeling ashamed.

"We've already learned that another word for ashamed is embarrassed. Other similar words are shy and humiliated. Shy isn't nearly as bad as feeling ashamed but feeling humiliated usually is worse than just being ashamed. If I spilled my lunch tray on my shirt in the cafeteria, I would feel ashamed and humiliated."

CHAPTER 4: PLACING WORDS IN CONTEXT

After the initial instruction of words, students need many and varied opportunities to interact with the new terms. To support the learning of target words, they should begin to build semantic, or word meaning, connections. The more that students can relate new words to existing knowledge, the more they'll be successful in integrating the content into their system of understanding (Blachowicz, Fisher, Ogle, & Watts-Taffe, 2006).

While the first few chapters of this book focused on teacher actions, specifically preparing for and presenting new vocabulary words, the remaining chapters look at student tasks. However, the goal of this and subsequent chapters is not to provide teachers with a source of worksheets to mindlessly throw at students. On the contrary, one of the primary methods that students should use to process what they've learned is conversation.

Sometimes, it is the discussion that goes along with trying to understand semantic relationships that has the most powerful impact on student learning (Blachowicz, Fisher, & Watts-Taffe, 2005). To get the most out of this reality, and to harness the motivational facet of relationships (read more about student motivation in appendix 3), teachers can do several things. They can structure opportunities for students to hear more academic language and hear words analyzed in an enjoyable way. Students should also practice using new academic language themselves (Kelley, Lesaux, Kieffer, & Faller, 2010).

A principal method of promoting these discussions is designing collaborative learning activities. As students work to place the new words into their existing bank of knowledge, their natural inclination is to interact with their peers. Not only does it stimulate language and metacognitive development, it's also a lot of fun!

Activating Prior Knowledge

Both neuroscience and vocabulary research agree – a key to quality vocabulary instruction is to tie new words into what students already know (Nagy & Herman, 1984). This is crucial because we usually learn something new by relating it to something that we already know. When a word definition uses information that is unknown to us, the results are less than ideal. See the two definitions below as an example:

> macaronic: composed of or characterized by Latin words mixed with vernacular words or non-Latin words given Latin endings
>
> macaronic: composed of a mixture of languages

The first definition assumes that you are familiar with the idea of romance languages (i.e., Latin words) and the term *vernacular*. If either of those items are not a part of your prior knowledge, then the first definition is not very useful. The second definition does a much better job, on the other hand, of relating the term *macaronic* to something most people know about – a mixture.

In the same way, sound vocabulary instruction includes the integration of what can be reasonably assumed to be the prior knowledge of students. While some students work well alone, others need social interactions to fully stimulate their critical thinking. Semantic maps, which show graphical relationships between word meanings, are a research-based practice that helps students acquire new word meanings

(Blachowicz, Fisher, Ogle, & Watts-Taffe, 2006; Nagy, 1988; Pythian-Sence & Wagner, 2007).

Word Association

An activity that students can utilize to tap into their wells of knowledge is called word association. In this free-flowing task, students work in pairs or in groups of three to write down as many words as they can think of that are related to the vocabulary word (Marzano & Pickering, 2005; Smith, 1997). Not necessarily restricted to synonyms only, word association helps place a new term in an established network of ideas.

Students should keep the word association list for possible use with other semantic maps. Teachers can also place a time limit, such as 30 seconds, on the word association activity. Students can go around in a larger circle (e.g., group of 4 to 6) and each name something associated with the target word. Like the game Hot Potato, the last person to speak when the timer goes off has to explain how his/her word is related to the target word.

Word Association can be done with little or no support for students in grade 3 or up. Students with limited ability and/or fluency with writing words might be too bogged down trying to spell the words to benefit from this exercise. Primary teachers can act as scribes so that student attention is focused on word association, not spelling.

Three Strikes and You're Down

For teachers that want to brainstorm word associations and share them as a class, a sharing technique can be used that keeps conversation moving without draining too much class time (Echevarria, Frey, & Fisher, 2016). Any educator that has ever conducted a class brainstorming session knows that unless properly managed, it can quickly turn into chaos or take much longer than necessary.

Called Three Strikes and You're Down, this strategy asks students to work in partners or in small groups to come up with as many words related to a target word as possible within a short amount of time. Instead of a group list, however, each student must keep his/her own list of related words. Then, teachers have each student stand up and they begin to share their words one at a time.

As each word is shared, the teacher creates a class list on chart paper or on the board. If a word is said by a student and other students have it on their papers, they cross the word off. When they've crossed off three words (i.e., three strikes), they sit down even if they haven't shared a word yet. This greatly reduces the sharing time while letting everyone participate.

This technique also has the effect of validating students' feelings of competence. Seeing that others have the same words as them lets them know that they are on the right track. Without a long and drawn out sharing session, students get visual and auditory confirmation of their own answers. The words that are not quickly shared, that perhaps might be unrelated or thinly related, provide an opportunity for the teacher to briefly discuss the merits of the questionable terms.

Again, younger students will need support to fully utilize this strategy. Instead of looking at it as one activity, primary teachers can break it up into two parts. The first part, generating lists of related words, can be done with teacher or peer support in small groups or centers. After each student has his/her own list, the class can be brought together to share using the Three Strikes and You're Down method.

Semantic Maps

The purpose of creating semantic maps is to help students gain a refined usage of new vocabulary. By highlighting subtle distinctions between related words, students can discover nuances of meaning that previously remained hidden. In addition, adding a new term to an established network of related words is easier than learning something entirely new without any connections. Word learning benefits greatly from the use of graphic organizers (e.g., semantic maps) to help restructure definitional information (Scott & Nagy, 2009).

Semantic maps gain much of their effectiveness by utilizing student motivation. They directly involve students in constructing meaning and allow students to freely associate words (Mebarki, 2011). Not only do word relationships become clearer, students feel valued that their prior knowledge plays such a large part in the process.

Some consider word learning to occur in two stages (Blachowicz, Fisher, & Watts-Taffe, 2005). In the first stage, a new word is identified and assigned to a broad semantic category. The second stage of word learning, then, is characterized by knowing more than a single definition of a word. Deep learning occurs when students have varied and rich experiences with the term. More importantly, they understand subdued differences within the semantic field between the target word and other words.

Synonym Web

One of the simplest semantic maps for students to create is a synonym web. Students work together to come up with as many synonyms of a target word as they can. They then build a web that groups synonyms based on shades of meaning for more complex words (Blachowicz, Fisher, & Watts-Taffe, 2005; Mebarki, 2011). For teachers of language arts, examining alternatives for the word *said* is a common practice.

Figure 4 is a fairly complex web. Until students become familiar with the process, their webs might only have one or two branches. In addition, it would be prudent to include a discard pile for words that do not fit neatly onto the web. Trying to wrestle every word into a category can result in warping the meaning of words beyond their true definitions.

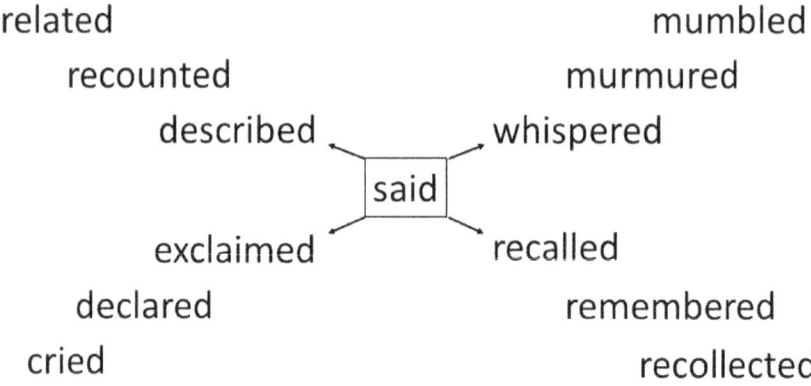

Figure 4: Synonym Web

Synonym/Antonym Continuum

A related semantic map, effective for older students, involves synonyms and/or antonyms. This should involve more than simply identifying similar and dissimilar words, however. Instead, students can evaluate words along a continuum of synonyms and antonyms. This will not only improve student understanding of word nuance, it will also have the benefit of improving their word choice in writing (Blachowicz, Fisher, & Watts-Taffe, 2005; Phillips, Foote, & Harper, 2008).

Take, for instance, the word *tepid.* Students can collaborate together to brainstorm a list of words that have to do with *tepid*. They might be synonyms, antonyms, or simply words that are otherwise related. Working together, they could come up with a list of synonyms and antonyms for *tepid* using prior knowledge, personal experiences, and even outside resources (e.g., thesaurus).

> lukewarm, hot, cold, cool, warm, room temperature, scorching, freezing

The analysis comes from placing these words along a continuum with *tepid* being the focal point. The closer that the words are to the focal point, the closer they are to being a synonym of *tepid*. An example can be seen in Figure 5.

Synonym/Antonym Continuum

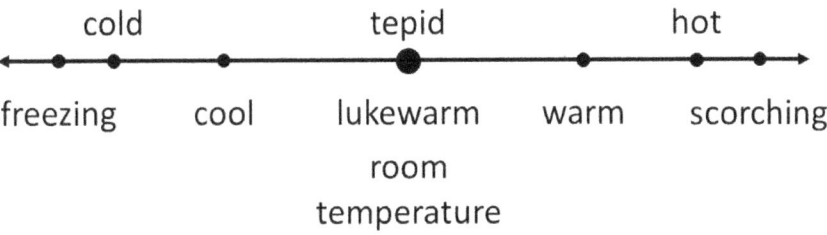

Figure 5: Synonym/Antonym Continuum

Using the word *tepid* as the focal point, antonyms existed at either extreme of the continuum. If the word only allowed for antonyms in one direction (e.g., using the word *scorching* as the vocabulary focal point), the continuum would still work. Instead of the focal point being in the center, however, it would be at one end or the other.

Concept of Definition Map

Another type of semantic map that has been successful in building word knowledge is a Concept of Definition Map (Blachowicz, Fisher, Ogle, & Watts-Taffe, 2006; Fisher, Frey, & Hattie, 2016; Smith, 1997). Using this map, students display hierarchical, categorical, and semantic information. Related to a word under consideration, students answer three questions. What is it? What is it like? What are some examples?

The first category seeks to define the term in student-friendly words. If studying the word *mollusk*, science students would define it as an invertebrate with a soft, unsegmented body that lives in damp or aquatic habitats.

The second category asks students to provide characteristics of the term to better understand it. Again referring to *mollusk*, students would brainstorm various descriptions of mollusks they know from reading and prior knowledge. They might produce phrases such as *usually has a shell*, *muscular foot*, and *mantle*.

Finally, students produce examples of the target term in order to place it within their network of existing knowledge. Instead of a completely unknown term, the purpose of the last category is to firmly relate the new term with prior experience. Students might give such examples as snails, squids, clams, and octopuses.

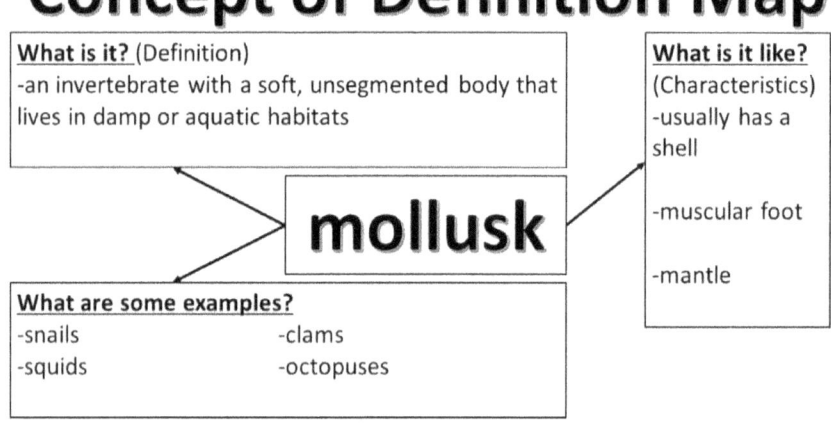

Figure 6: Concept of Definition Map

Hierarchical Map

Some relationships are best displayed in a hierarchy or taxonomy. A colt, for example, is a young male horse that is less than four years old. That can be contrasted with a filly, a young female horse. Young horses of either sex can be called foals if they are less than a year old and yearlings if they between one and two years old. It is these relationships that help further add meaning to the target word *colt*.

Another type of semantic map that can be explored by students, then, is a hierarchical map (Nagy, 1988). When related words can be displayed in a hierarchy and relationships are defined by their place in the structure, it helps students place new words within existing knowledge.

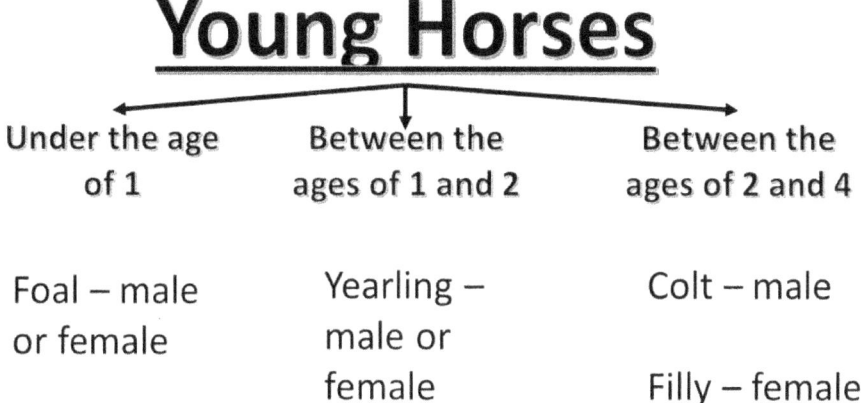

Figure 7: Hierarchical Map

Remember that the purpose of vocabulary instruction is to increase knowledge in general. By comparing the term *colt* to related terms and showing how they are alike and dissimilar, students will have a much clearer idea of what a *colt* is and is not. Another consequence of creating semantic maps is that it exposes students to additional words not currently being studied. This can sometimes increase word knowledge even more if students become motivated by the subject.

Root Map

Students can also build understanding by taking a vocabulary word with a common root and exploring other uses of the same root. By concentrating on the analysis of the root word, students not only refine their understanding of that word but also extend it to related words (Blachowicz, Fisher, & Watts-Taffe, 2005).

For example, students studying the words from *The Ugly Duckling* should notice that *joyously* and *joyfully* both contain the root word *joy*.

Building on that, they can brainstorm or research using the dictionary or online tools some other words with the same root. A list of those words might include: joy, joyously, joyfully, joyful, enjoy, enjoyable, enjoyment, joyride, joyless, overjoy, unenjoyable, killjoy, and joystick.

Students then can work to group the terms together using similarities in meaning, grammar usage, or some other characteristic. If looking at the group of brainstormed words and grouping them together by meaning, the resulting semantic map would look similar to the one below.

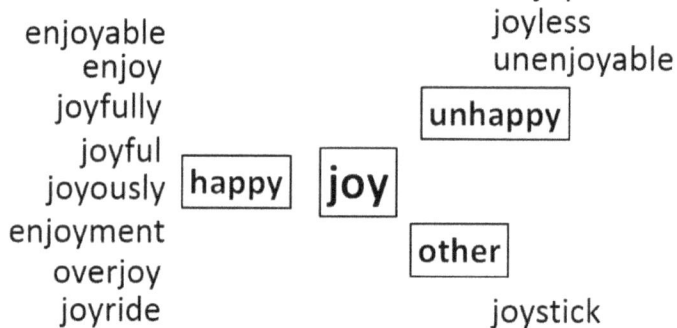

Figure 8: Meaning Root Map

Another way to group the words, however, would be to do so by parts of speech. Mapping the words by grammar usage would allow the students to examine the words in a completely different light (Figure 9).

The study of word roots or other parts, such as affixes, allows for students to expand their word knowledge beyond the words currently under study. It makes them sensitive to word analysis and gives them the tools needed to uncover the meanings of related words.

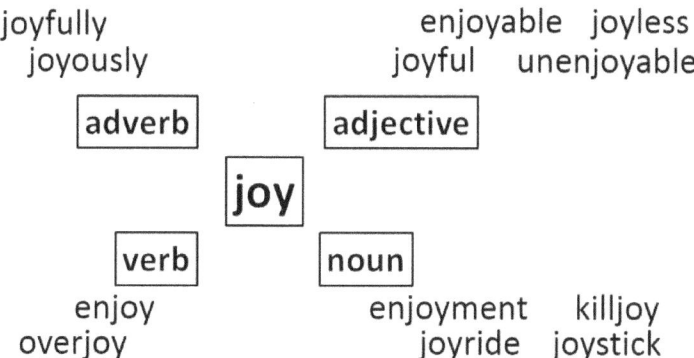

Figure 9: Usage Root Map

In general, words are semantically related in three ways: synonymy, antonymy, and morphology (Blachowicz, Fisher, & Watts-Taffe, 2005). Comparing and contrasting related words helps students develop a sensitivity to word meanings (Nagy, 1988). Instruction that involves activating prior knowledge, in addition to comparing and contrasting word meanings, is more powerful than simply providing definitional and contextual information alone (Graves, 2015/2016).

Chapter 5: Basic Processing Tasks (Mastery/Understanding)

After vocabulary words are presented through direct instruction and placed into existing webs of knowledge through semantic maps, students need multiple opportunities to process the new terms. This chapter and the following chapter specifically look at various activities that can engage students and help them add to the knowledge of each word. Complex understanding deepens over time if students continually reexamine their interpretations of studied words (Marzano & Pickering, 2005).

For vocabulary instruction to prove effective, it must promote deep processing and thoughtful reflections (Beck, McKeown, Wagner, Muse, & Tannenbaum, 2007; Nagy & Townsend, 2012). The more deeply information is processed, the more likely it is to be remembered. Meaningful, purposeful, and effective effort must be expended on the part of the student for word knowledge to blossom (Nagy, 1988). Students who wrestle with rather than memorize words greatly increase their recall and subsequent usage.

For this to happen, two components are essential. To begin with, memories are typically not made permanent after a single exposure.

Filling in a worksheet or studying a word for one week and never seeing it again will prove highly ineffective. Instead, students need multiple exposures over a long period of time (Graves, 2015/2016). The activities in this chapter and the next will be presented for processing newly learned words. Additionally, they should also be viewed as tools to keep previously studied words fresh in students' minds.

The second component that helps students to process words is discussion (Graves, Baumann, & Blachowicz, 2014). Even though most of the following activities could be turned into solitary assignments taken for a grade, much effectiveness would be lost with the transformation. As much or more learning takes place through the discussion during an activity than by simply completing the activity itself. Encouraging conversation allows students a safe area to try out new ideas and attempt to make meaning of unknown terms without worrying about grades.

All processing tasks are not equal, however. Stahl and Fairbanks (1986) cite three levels of the depth of processing demands. The first, or lowest, level is associative. Students learn to relate or associate the new word with a definition or within a single context. The second, or middle, level is comprehension. Children working at this level show their understanding in a sentence or by doing something with definitional information. This could be finding an antonym or classifying words based on semantic properties.

The third, or highest, level is generation. Processing tasks at this level demand that students produce novel responses about or including the vocabulary terms. This could be an original sentence, a restatement of the definition in the child's own words, or an original written or oral response. Drill-and-kill vocabulary tasks that rely heavily on multiple low-level repetitions (i.e., level one associative) do not produce a reliable effect on reading comprehension (Stahl & Fairbanks, 1986).

This chapter and the following chapter will look exclusively at level two comprehension processing tasks while chapter 7 examines level three generative tasks. The method used to organize the following level two activities will be through the lens of learning styles (Silver, Strong, & Perini, 2007): mastery, understanding, interpersonal, and self-expressive. The first two will be used to examine processing tasks in this chapter while the last two will be poured over in chapter 6.

Mastery learners do best when remembering and summarizing. They enjoy clear sequences, expanding competence, and measurable success. These learners prefer tasks such as to-do lists and memorization. For the most part, the traditional education system is built for these types of learners. Of all the students that populate classrooms across the country, mastery learners are the most likely to enjoy fill-in-the-blank worksheets.

Understanding learners, however, prefer using reason and logic. Mysteries that invoke their curiosity and opportunities to analyze and debate are highly motivational. These learners prefer to know why something works rather than simply performing a task or remembering a fact. They relish the opportunity to explore the nuances of word meanings and enjoy analyzing context and grammar usage.

Mastery Processing Tasks

The following level two comprehension tasks are appropriate for all learners but focus on definitional mastery. Students participating in these activities will validate and expand their understanding of the target words. Mastery learners will find particular joy in working through tasks designed to increase their competence.

Questioning

One of the most effective methods of processing knowledge is to answer questions about the vocabulary words themselves (Blachowicz, Fisher, & Watts-Taffe, 2005; Brief, 2008; Fisher, Frey, & Hattie, 2016; Graves, Baumann, & Blachowicz, 2014; Nagy, 1988). The types of questions to be answered, however, should be much more than simple definitional queries. Instead, students can look for semantic relationships by making inferences (Nagy, 1988) and that require deep thinking (Graves, Baumann, & Blachowicz, 2014).

The type of questions can also vary (Brief, 2008). They can be questions involving a single word or multiple words at once. Another type of inferential thinking can be true/false statements that students interact with. How students respond to the questions should differ as well. They can discuss with a partner or group, write down their thoughts in a journal, or hold up response cards (e.g, True/False, Yes/No).

"Alright, students, I have a few questions for you. Now that we've reread The Ugly Duckling and have studied the vocabulary words and built some semantic maps, I'm going to ask you a few things about our terms. Each of you will work with a partner and have a Yes/No paddle. After I ask each question, quietly talk with your partner to decide on your answer and then hold up the side of the paddle that shows your choice. Ready? Here we go.

"Would you feel *persecuted* if a bully was picking on you?

"Would you *despise* your favorite aunt?

"Would you describe a ballerina as *graceful*?

"Would you feel *sorrow* at your birthday party?

"Now I'm going to pass out some True/False paddles. I'll read some statements that include two or more vocabulary words. If the statement makes sense, hold up the side that says True. If one or more of the words have been used incorrectly and it doesn't make sense, hold up the side that says False.

"The thief felt *joyous* at being *persecuted* by the police detective.

"The deer *rustled* the branches as it walked past the *slender* tree.

"The team captain's eyes filled with *sorrow* as the *despised* crosstown rival won the city championship.

"The boy *joyfully stroked* the fur of the wild mountain cat.

"Finally, please open up your vocabulary journals and look at the copy of the questions and statements we've just looked at as a class. Choose one question or statement that was wrong and write how you would fix it. Make sure to explain why the statement or question is incorrect and how you would fix it. If you decide to change a word, the new word doesn't have to be a vocabulary word."

Sentence Completion

Similar to answering questions about vocabulary words, students can also complete sentences about descriptions that involve various terms (Brief, 2008). This technique can be approached using two different methods, both of which are important. First, teachers can give students a sentence that provides definitional context for a vocabulary term and ask students to supply the correct word. Conversely, teachers can provide a vocabulary term within context and ask students to finish the sentence using descriptive terms.

Flexibility of language use comes from repeated exposures in a variety of contexts. Instead of simply utilizing one approach, such as filling in the correct term, students should approach vocabulary from a multitude of perspectives. Word knowledge is more than simply bubbling in the correct definition on an exam. The aim of vocabulary is to help students not only answer questions about words but use them in daily communication.

"Let's take a look at some sentences I've created about our vocabulary words," Mr. Wilson said to the class. "In this first set, there will be a missing word at the end that will make the sentence complete. The answer will be one of the vocabulary words and please pay attention to grammar usage. If the word is an adjective, it'll be used as an adjective. If you get stuck, feel free to ask your partner for help.

"Someone who is grumpy and doesn't want to do what anyone else suggests is …

"Someone who feels like everyone is always watching them and making fun of them feels …

"Something that is smooth and fluid can be described as …

"Something that is thin and elegant can be described as …

"Now that you've had a chance to complete those sentences, I'm going to change them up a little bit. I'll provide the beginning of a sentence and you need to complete it using what you know about the word. The sentences can be finished however you want but the more descriptive it is of the word, the better. Please record each of your completed sentences in your vocabulary journal. After we are done, you'll share your sentences with your group and decide which one best describes each word.

"Someone who feels *sorrow* would say …

"Someone who acts *joyously* would …

"Someone who is *despised* would probably …

"When something is *rustled* it sounds like …

"Read your completed sentences with your group and explain your thinking as to why you chose the words you did. Work together to choose the best sentence for each sentence stem that describes what the word means using powerful language. We will share those as a class and select a few to add to our class vocabulary notebook."

Frayer Model

A third technique that teachers can employ to encourage vocabulary processing for mastery learners is by using the Frayer method (Fisher, Frey, & Hattie, 2016). It asks students to evaluate and expand on word knowledge from a variety of angles. This multi-dimensional approach helps students connect prior knowledge to target vocabulary by utilizing multiple types of connections.

In the traditional Frayer model, students split a piece of notebook or journal paper into four quadrants. After writing the vocabulary word in the middle, students write a definition in the upper left-hand quadrant. This definition should be in the student's own words rather than a sterile dictionary definition. For struggling students, teachers can provide a definition with simplified language.

The upper right-hand quadrant is where students record characteristics of the target term. They should focus on features that help students identify the word and what distinguishes it from other related words. The lower left-hand quadrant is for examples while the lower right-hand quadrant is for non-examples. They can be synonyms (examples) or antonyms (non-examples), correct or incorrect applications, or even illustrations. The non-examples should stand in contrast to the target word rather than being something completely unrelated and random.

Frayer models take some time and thought and, unless the vocabulary list is small, students will probably not have time to complete one for every term. Instead, this provides an opportunity for teachers to leverage the motivational facet of autonomy and allow students the chance to choose which words to explore with a Frayer model. For example, if students are studying eight words that week, the teacher can ask them to choose four terms and create a Frayer model for each one. This will allow students to exercise choice select which words to explore. Teachers will also be surprised by how many students decide to complete more than the four required diagrams simply because it's their choice to do so.

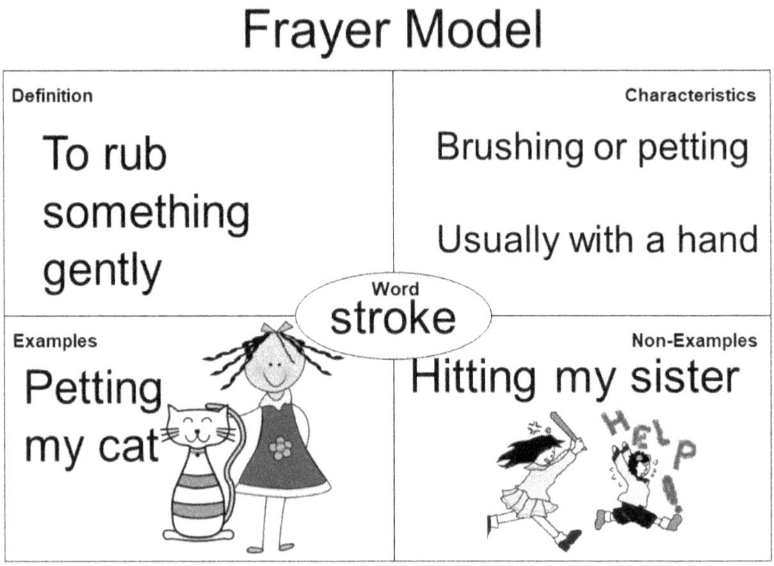

Frayer Model

Definition	Characteristics
To rub something gently	Brushing or petting Usually with a hand
Examples Petting my cat	**Non-Examples** Hitting my sister

Word: stroke

Figure 10: Frayer Model

Understanding Processing Tasks

The following level two processing tasks ask students to use logic and reasoning to evaluate words and their semantic relationships. As with the mastery tasks, they are appropriate for all students but will highly motivate those that are drawn to puzzles, mysteries, and using deductive reasoning.

Solving Analogies

Analogous thinking is a solid processing task that asks students to identify and interpret the relationships between words (Marzano & Pickering, 2005; Smith, 1997). A key part of activity is understanding the relating factor that ties the two words together. When considering analogies, most adults tend to think about the kinds of problems given to high school students on the SAT test. For example, a typical question is set up like this:

Choose the answer that best matches the analogy:

walk:legs

    A. *gleam:eyes*

    B. *chew:mouth*

    C. *dress:hem*

    D. *cover:book*

    E. *grind:nose*

The key to finding the answer is to analyze the relationship between the original pair. Students at a young age can be trained to evaluate analogies if shown how to verbalize the relationships between words. Using the example above, students should place the two words in a sentence that explains how they are related. They might come up with something akin to "you walk with your legs."

Taking that simple phrase, students then substitute the other pairs and evaluate their reasonableness. Using this method, they can quickly see that the best answer is B because "you chew with your mouth." For students to solve analogies, teachers should set them up with increasingly difficult and varied relationships. Some different relationships that teachers can utilize are shown in the table on the next page.

    Mr. Wilson wanted his students to process the vocabulary words they were studying by analyzing their relationships with other words. To do this, he set up a series of analogies that involved one or more vocabulary terms. Since this type of thinking was new to most of the students, he began to explain how students could use reasoning to correctly answer analogy questions.

Table 2: Analogy Relationships

Type	Relationship	Example
Synonym	is similar to	happy:glad
Antonym	is the opposite of	anger:joy
Part to Whole	is a part of	hand:body
Category	is a type of	dog:mammal
Object-Function	is used to	scale:weigh
Person-Action	does/performs	boxer:fights
Cause-Effect	is a cause of	poison oak:rash

"Class, today we are going to look at something called an analogy. Analogies are used to describe relationships between words. An analogy typically has two parts that use the same relationship. Let's look at an example – dog:bark. How would you describe the relationship between dog and bark?"

A student raised her hand and said, "Dogs bark."

Mr. Wilson replied, "That is correct. Barking is something that dogs do. Another way to say it would be the noise a dog makes is called a bark. The next part of the analogy then needs to match that same relationship. Here are the possible matches – cat:fur, giraffe:long neck, zebra:stripes, lion:roar."

The students worked in pairs and evaluated each possible answer. They quickly reached a conclusion and Mr. Wilson called on one student to share her answer.

"We think the answer is the last one – lion:roar. The other three all describe what that animal looks like but the last one is the only one that says what kind of noise the animal makes," the student answered.

"Great answer," Mr. Wilson responded. "Once you've decided on the relationship between the first half of the analogy, you look for a matching pair that uses that same relationship. Would you like to try some more analogies using your vocabulary words from The Ugly Duckling?" The children all agreed and excitedly began to examine the new analogies.

Synonym Feature Analysis

Synonym feature analysis, sometimes called semantic feature analysis, requires students to delve deep into the nuances between word meanings (Blachowicz, Fisher, & Watts-Taffe, 2005; Nagy, 1988). The primary goal is to add texture to target word meanings by differentiating between denotations (e.g., literal meanings) and connotations (e.g., suggested meanings) of various synonyms. By evaluating related words, students add depth and complexity to their understanding of vocabulary words.

One method of analyzing synonyms is to use a sample sentence (Blachowicz, Fisher, & Watts-Taffe, 2005). To begin with, a single vocabulary word should be chosen, either by the teacher or the student, as the subject of analysis. Then, either by brainstorming, the use of a thesaurus, or both, a list of synonyms should be created. Keep in mind that the synonyms should be words that students know and are comfortable with.

The next part is the creation of the sample sentence. It should be fairly simple yet descriptive of the vocabulary word. Students will read the sample sentence multiple times, each time substituting a synonym for the vocabulary word and discussing how the connotative interpretations change with each new word.

For example, students might perform a synonym feature analysis with the word *slender*. Appropriate synonyms are *thin, delicate, fragile, lanky, narrow, skinny,* and *wiry*. A sample sentence might be created that mirrors the term's use in the original passage: *The swan curved its slender neck.* Students would then read the sentence multiple times, each time inserting a synonym for *slender*.

The swan curved its slender neck.

The swan curved its thin neck.

The swan curved its delicate neck.

The swan curved its fragile neck.

The swan curved its lanky neck.

The swan curved its narrow neck.

The swan curved its skinny neck.

The swan curved its wiry neck.

It is the conversations that students hold while conducting a synonym feature analysis that hold the greatest potential for learning. They should recognize that though all the synonyms have similar denotative meanings, their connotations greatly affect the meaning of each sentence.

While the terms *thin, lanky, narrow, skinny,* and *wiry* all carry the implication of being slim, several of those terms carry an arguably negative connotation. The words *thin, lanky,* and *skinny* are not nearly as graceful as the original word *slender. Narrow* is a more neutral term but still lacks the elegance of *slender*.

Students should also notice that the terms *fragile* and *delicate* carry a different connotation, that of being breakable. While that meaning is not evident in the original text, it adds depth to the word *slender*.

Students should discuss that sometimes a lack of thickness is associated with being easily broken.

Another variation on the use of sample sentences is constructing a synonym feature matrix (Nagy, 1988). Instead of using a sample sentence, students construct a table with the synonyms in the first column and various attributes in the remaining columns.

Table 3: Synonym Feature Matrix

	not fat	graceful	breakable	weak	long
slender	+	+	?	?	?
thin	+	?	?	?	?
delicate	?	?	+	?	?
fragile	?	-	+	+	?
lanky	+	?	?	-	+
narrow	+	?	?	?	?
skinny	+	?	?	?	?
wiry	+	?	-	-	?

For example, students can evaluate *slender* and the aforementioned synonyms against five possible connotations: not fat, graceful, breakable, weak, and long. If students believe the synonym positively describes the characteristic, they should put a "+" in the corresponding box. If they are not sure or if the characteristic does not indicate positive or negative correlation, they can place a "?" in the box. If the synonyms suggests the opposite of the characteristic, the students can place a "-" in the box (see Table 3).

As with the other activities and strategies presented in this book, the work being done by students will by nature be subjective. Emphasis should be placed on quality conversations and deep processing rather than finding a correct answer. Most vocabulary work does not need to be formally assessed or graded because the word growth, not a potential piece of information for the gradebook, is the focus.

Something to keep when mind when considering the usefulness of synonym feature analysis is the general vocabulary sophistication of the students. This processing task requires a base level of work knowledge to be successful, as it focuses on slight variations in meaning. Younger students or those with limited vocabulary knowledge would be hampered by their unfamiliarity with the synonyms of the target word.

Chapter 6: Basic Processing Tasks (Interpersonal/Self-Expressive)

When considering student learning styles, various questions can be used to encapsulate what each type of learner seeks to understand. Mastery learners are most concerned with questions like, "What?" They want to know the correct answer and what they need to do to show their competence. Understanding learners, however, are more driven by questions like, "Why?" Instead of simply knowing the solution, they seek to know why those solutions work. Mastery and understanding processing tasks were examined in chapter 5.

The third type of learning style is interpersonal and these students are driven by questions like, "Who?" Interpersonal learners thrive while utilizing their social prowess. They learn best when relating the content to themselves and others. Teams, cooperative learning, and even coaching motivate them through the energy they derive from relationships. These learners would rather read a story about someone in history than perusing a dusty history textbook.

Finally, self-expressive learners prefer to use their imagination and creativity. They are constantly asking "What if?" and trying new ideas out. Imagery, metaphors, and patterns motivate them to express their individuality and originality. These learners not only want to know how something works, they want to tweak it and make it their own.

Interpersonal Processing Tasks

Although all of the processing tasks in chapters 5-7 include a relational component, the next few tasks are designed specifically for the interpersonal learning style. These activities are built around student interaction and harness social cooperation for academic purposes.

Think-Pair-Square

In the traditional think-pair-share strategy, students are given a question or prompt to consider. After appropriate think time, students pair up and share their answers or thoughts with each other (Marzano & Pickering, 2005). Taking that foundation and adding an additional component, interpersonal learners will find much value in a strategy called think-pair-square (Echevarria, Frey, & Fisher, 2016).

To fully utilize social interactions, students should be given a powerful prompt to think about during the first part of this processing task. Instead of asking students to think about a word, they should be given a more specific cue to consider. Some possible questions are:

- What are some descriptive examples of your word?
- How would you define your word to a friend who has never heard it before?
- How would you use your word in a sentence so that its meaning could be understood from the sentence itself?
- If you were to draw a picture to describe your word, what would that look like?
- What are some objects that could represent your word? Why did you choose them?

After sufficient think time, students should next pair up to share their thoughts. One thought about pairing, however. Teachers should have a pairing strategy already in mind before asking students to find a partner.

Typical pairings involve someone sitting next to or across from the student. Asking students to simply find a partner in the room can quickly turn into a chaotic free-for-all.

When sharing their thoughts with their partners, students should practice active listening and questioning. They should ask follow-up questions for clarification and require their partners to explain their reasoning. The final part of the strategy has each pair of students find another pair to form a square. In the square, pairs share their responses with the other pair.

A key way to build on the interpersonal strengths of learners is to have students share their partner's response in the square rather than their own responses. If they know that they will be required to represent someone else's responses, they will be encouraged to pay close attention. Students will also ask more probing questions in order to better understand what they will be reporting later.

Inside/Outside Circle

Another technique that can be utilized to encourage student interactions is an inside/outside circle (Echevarria, Frey, & Fisher, 2016). To easily facilitate productive conversations, students form two concentric circles. A quick way to form the circles is to have the entire class form one large circle and number off starting at one. The students with the odd numbers will form the outer circle. The students with the even numbers will take one step inward and turn around to form the inner circle.

With the two circles formed, students should make an inner-outer pair. It is at this point that the teacher should direct the students to respond to vocabulary-related questions with their partners. They can give synonyms to a certain word, provide a descriptive definition, or generate real-word examples.

After each partner has responded, the teacher will direct either the inner or outer circle to rotate in a certain direction. For example, the teacher could tell the inner circle to move two places to the left or the outer circle to move three places to the right. Once one of the circles has moved, the teacher can ask another question or give another prompt.

This deceptively simple strategy motivates students in several ways. First, movement energizes the body and increases positive emotions. It builds relationships with students and allows them to build competence by trying out their answers in a risk-free (i.e., not graded) setting. Finally, it changes the pace of the lesson by providing a bit of mystery to the lesson. Some students will want to participate simply to see who their next partner will be!

Roundtable

For teachers that want to include a multi-faceted approach to word study, roundtable is a great strategy to incorporate (Echevarria, Frey, & Fisher, 2016). In groups of four, each student folds a piece of paper into four quadrants. They each then fold a triangle in the corner of the paper with two folds. When unfolded, it opens up so that is looks similar to a Frayer model but with a diamond in the middle (Figure 11).

There are many different variations of this collaborative technique that teachers can use to encourage students to process vocabulary words. One method is to assign four words to each group and have each student choose a different word. Students then write down their thoughts or give examples of the word in one of the quadrants.

After a short time, students rotate their papers and add their thoughts about a different word on a new paper. They should read what has already been shared and attempt to add to those thoughts rather than repeating them. When the papers have rotated three times, they return to the owner with all four quadrants filled. Students then use the central diamond to write a statement that synthesizes everyone's thoughts. If students have questions about what someone else wrote, they can ask for clarification.

An alternate form of this method is to assign one word each group.

After students fold their papers, they label the four quadrants like a Frayer model (Figure 12).

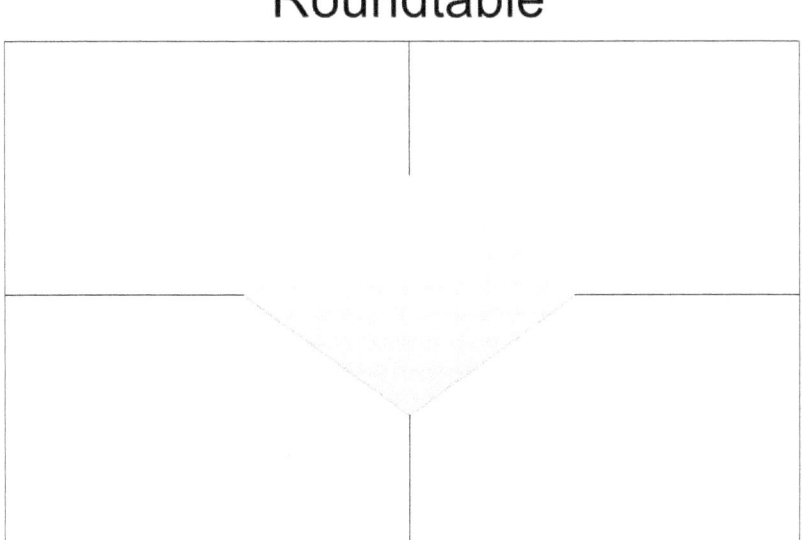

Figure 11: Roundtable

Students fill in one quadrant of their choice for the target word and then rotate the papers. After each rotation, students fill in a different quadrant of their choice. If possible, they should choose a new quadrant to fill out so that they are not completing the same section (e.g., examples) for four consecutive papers. After the papers have been returned, students once again write a synthesis statement in the central diamond.

With either method, or even a hybrid of the two, the purpose is to create a complex understanding of the word by utilizing the prior knowledge of peers. While the opportunity for misunderstandings does exist, clarifying questions and follow-up opportunities will encourage continued conversations about word meanings.

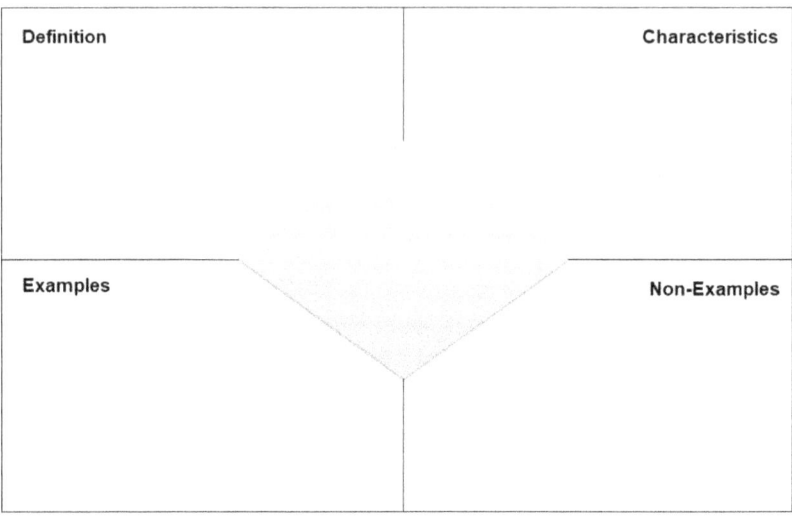

Figure 12: Roundtable Frayer Model

Self-Expressive Processing Tasks

In addition to mastery, understanding, and interpersonal processing tasks, some students would greatly benefit from unleashing their creativity. Self-expressive tasks encourage students to play with words and make judgments about their uses. As with other activities, the purpose is to encourage divergent thinking and semantic flexibility rather than finding a correct answer.

Free Association

A quick-and-easy processing activity that caters to self-expressive learners is called free association (Marzano & Pickering, 2005). It not only serves as a stand-alone activity, it can be completed in a vocabulary journal and used as a springboard for further processing tasks.

To complete free association, students are given a vocabulary term and a short amount of time (e.g., one minute) to write down as many words as they can think of that are related to the target word. While some students might be tempted to limit their thoughts to synonyms, the purpose is to expand their thinking beyond the obvious associations. In addition to words that are similar, students can list antonyms, examples, or even classifications or types.

Once students have made their lists, they switch with a partner. Partners should read over the new list and circle a few terms for further discussion. Partners might circle words they find interesting or those that they are confused about. Students then discuss their circled words with each other and provide clarification as needed.

Another permutation of free association, if students have sufficient experience with the task, is to ask partners to classify the freely associated words. For example, they might take their partner's terms and sort them into synonyms and antonyms. They could also organize them into words the partner knows and words the partner doesn't know. This would itself spawn a productive conversation between students about word meanings.

Keyword Method

One of the earliest and most documented methods to learning vocabulary terms is the mnemonic keyword method (Blachowicz, Fisher, & Watts-Taffe, 2005; Brief, 2008; Pressley, Disney, & Anderson, 2007; Pythian-Sence & Wagner, 2007; Stahl & Fairbanks, 1986). This strategy, named after the Greek word *mnema* which means *memory* (Tate, 2016), has students learn new terms by associating a part of the target word with something that is already known. This method has been studied and found to be more effective than similar semantic methods (Stahl & Fairbanks, 1986).

The keyword method uses both auditory and visual cues to enhance the learning of the word and its meanings (Blachowicz, Fisher, & Watts-Taffe, 2005). Students choose a familiar word or term that either lies within or closely resembles a part of the target word. This keyword is then illustrated to connect the keyword with the target word's meaning.

For example, consider the mathematical term *ray* that elementary students might encounter. A ray is a line that has a starting point but no endpoint. One way students might illustrate this term is to draw a picture of a man named Ray running a never-ending race. They illustrate that he has a beginning point but never quite reaches the end. The picture should include a student-friendly definition as well.

Figure 13: Keyword Method 1

Another example from elementary mathematics is the term *parallel*, which refers to lines that are the same distance apart and never intersect (Figure 14). The keyword for *parallel* would be its similarity to the phrase "pair of elves." Building on that, students can draw two parallel lines, include two elves, and write an understandable definition.

This method works well for some students because of how our memories work. It encodes information in multiple areas of the brain (i.e., visual, auditory, semantic) and greatly increases the chances of recall. While it does not necessarily provide deep analysis of words, it does allow self-expressive learners to explore their creativity. Instead of memorizing bland definitions, students will thrive with the opportunity to be creative.

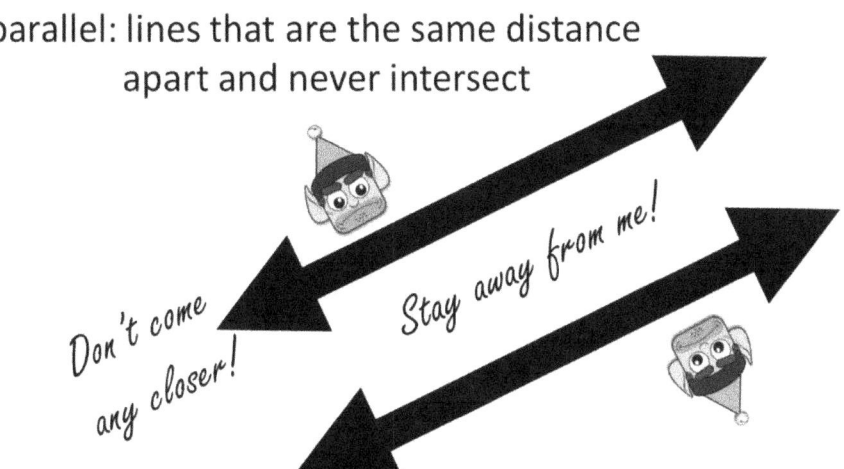

Figure 14: Keyword Method 2

Opinion Corners

Based on the strategy Opinion Stations (Echevarria, Frey, & Fisher, 2016), opinion corners works best if each corner of the classroom is labeled either Always Agree, Sometimes Agree, Sometimes Disagree, or Always Disagree. If the layout of the room prohibits this, tables or various sections of the room can be labeled instead. Using the list of vocabulary words, students would respond to various declarative statements created by the teacher.

The students then will have to evaluate their response to teacher statements. They move to the corner that most closely corresponds to their opinion (i.e., Always Agree, Sometimes Agree, Sometimes Disagree, or Always Disagree). When all students have chosen their corners, the students confer with those that have similar beliefs. They discuss their reasoning and work together to prepare their reasons with the class.

For those students in either extreme corner (i.e., Always Agree or Always Disagree), their purpose is to anticipate and plan for arguments dissuading them from their opinion. The two more central positions (i.e., Sometimes Agree, Sometimes Disagree) should seek to find fault in the opinions of the more extreme positions. These students are looking for examples to disprove an all-or-nothing position.

For this strategy to work, students need to be able to think outside the box, form cogent arguments, and know how to disagree in a respectful manner. As thoughts are shared with the class, students should be encouraged to change groups if they hear a compelling argument. Movement should be celebrated and the rationale for changing should be shared with the class. Instead of right or wrong answers, students work to hone their persuasive skills and learn how to have a respectful dialogue.

Using the words from *The Ugly Duckling*, some example sentences are:

- A *slender* stick will break easily.
- *Persecuted* people feel anger and helplessness.
- *Sorrow* is a negative emotion.
- Students who argue are *disagreeable*.
- Ballerinas are *graceful*.
- Someone who wins the lottery would be *joyful*.

As with previous processing tasks, the thought processes and conversations that take place between students is much more important than generating specific answers. Forming and dissecting arguments asks students to relate the statements to their own experiences. In the process of justifying the opinion corner they chose, they are also integrating the term into the context of their prior knowledge.

By using opinion corners, students have an opportunity to safely test out their thoughts without fear of getting something wrong. Being able to move to a different corner based on persuasive arguments allows students the freedom to take risks and evaluate their answers without penalty. This particular strategy can generate strong emotions as students, hopefully respectfully, argue about their choices. This will create further connections to the word's meaning as it becomes associated with emotional experiences.

Chapter 7: Complex Processing Tasks

While level two comprehension tasks ask students to evaluate various vocabulary words, level three generative tasks are much more open-ended. These activities provoke students to engineer their own novel responses. Whereas the previous two chapters' tasks sorted themselves by a single learning style, the following level three tasks are multi-faceted and incorporate all four learning styles.

One thought to keep in mind is that level three generation processing tasks are not necessarily more valuable than level two comprehension processing tasks. Instead, they demand a different type of thought pattern and should be used progressively. Students must first comprehend a word in a variety of ways (level two tasks) before they can use it independently (level three tasks).

Response Stems

An easy-to-use generative task is called response stems (Blachowicz, Fisher, & Watts-Taffe, 2005). Students take the beginning of sentences that target a particular word and complete them on their own. This can be done verbally or can be written down in vocabulary journals. Regardless of the method used to interact with response stems, the conversations that accompany the task are critical. Response stems are similar in makeup to sentence completion (chapter 5). The difference lies in the rubric component, discussed below, of response stems and the possibility for largely varied responses.

Good response stems should target specific characteristics or senses. For example, ask students where something would take place or what they would do in a certain situation. Students can also complete a response stem with what they would say, feel, or even hear in response to a word. As with most open-ended tasks, they require a strong rubric to guide student responses.

If students were responding to a stem such as, "Someone who is *persecuted* would say...", there should be a framework that helps them generate deeper sentences. This framework can be posted and used as a reference for students as they generate their responses. The use of a posted rubric provides reflective feedback for students and allows them a clear path toward improvement.

While simple sentences will successfully satisfy the requirements of this task, students should be encouraged to expand their writing to multiple sentences to fully flesh out their thoughts. Students should respond to the stems and then evaluate their own work using a rubric like the one on the following page. With enough practice, students can begin to craft detailed sentences or even paragraphs in response to a simple response stem.

The correct frame of mind for students to embody during this task is not one of completion but of explanation. Their goal is not to simply satisfy the requirements of the task but to expand their response to the fullest extent possible. With quality response stems, the possibilities are endless.

Mastery learners will benefit most from using the rubric. With something as open-ended as response stems, students who value growing their competence need structure. Using a rubric allows for these students to take the vagueness of a subjective task and give it some order.

Table 4: Response Stem Rubric

Response Stem Rubric

Level	Description	Example
0	The response does not explain what the word means.	When I feel *disagreeable* I go to my room.
1	The response somewhat explains what the word means.	When I feel *disagreeable* I am angry.
2	The response explains what the word means.	When I feel *disagreeable* I am in a bad mood and no one wants to be around me.
3	The response fully explains what the word means with an example.	When I feel *disagreeable* I am unpleasant and don't enjoy things. If my friend suggests something to do, I say, "That's boring."
4	The response fully explains what the word means using multiple examples or perspectives.	When I feel *disagreeable* I snap at people for no reason. No idea is good enough and people usually avoid me. It's like I have a rain cloud over my head.

Understanding learners, on the other hand, will be most drawn to level 3 and level 4 responses. They will relish the opportunity to show their comprehension of the word by generating sentences that are complex and informative. Their responses might be the most perceptive and nuanced in the class.

Interpersonal learners would benefit from working with a partner after the responses have been generated. In addition to a self-assessment using the rubric, some students would gain much from getting feedback from a peer. If the original sentence does not rank high enough on the rubric, they can work collaboratively to improve their response.

Finally, self-expressive learners will benefit most from the open-ended nature of the task. While understanding learners might deliver the deepest responses, these learners will most likely generate the most creative. A task like this allows them to think outside the box rather than hemming them in with worksheets and fill-in-the-blank assignments.

Acrostics

Simple Acrostic
Sad
Out of sorts
Remorse
Regret
Oppressed
Worry

Figure 15: Simple Acrostic

Students can also generate deep and meaningful interpretations of vocabulary words by creating acrostics (Tate, 2016). An acrostic, put simply, is a set of words, phrases, or sentences that revolve around a central word. Each letter of the word is used in a word or phrase to describe the term itself.

While simple to explain and fairly common even in elementary grades, acrostics allow for many permutations and levels of support. Simple acrostics use the first letter in the target word to stand for the first letter in multiple words that each describe the word under consideration.

Acrostic sentences, on the other hand, utilize the same structure but attempt to form a sentence or series of sentences describing the target word. Rather than each letter of the target word standing alone, acrostic sentences should be read in one fluid reading as you would a paragraph.

Acrostic Sentence

<u>D</u>on't just
<u>E</u>xclaim, "I don't like it."
<u>S</u>ome things deserve no
<u>P</u>ity or sympathy.
<u>I</u>rate feelings of resentment
<u>S</u>erve to show your attitude toward
<u>E</u>verything you truly loathe.

Figure 16: Acrostic Sentence

Finally, some students might struggle with the creation of either simple acrostics or acrostic sentences. A modified version of typical acrostics allows students to use any letter in the descriptive words to match up to the letters of the target word. This adjustment works both for simple acrostics and acrostic sentences.

Regardless of the type of acrostics students work on, they should be encouraged to explore their creativity in a way that is comfortable to them. To ease students in the acrostic making process, ready access to a thesaurus, either print or online, should be available.

Mastery learners will be drawn more to the simple acrostic with its clear layout and no-nonsense function. Though some might view it as more difficult than a modified acrostic, mastery learners will appreciate the simplicity of its design.

Modified Acrostic

eleGant
limbeR
beaAutiful
deliCate
Exquisite
graceFul
sUpple
Lithe

Figure 17: Modified Acrostic

Understanding learners like to explore why things are true rather than just learning cold facts. They will enjoy the symmetry of using a word as a structure for defining itself. Understanding learners will most likely gravitate toward acrostic sentences as they seek to explain their target words with in-depth examples.

Interpersonal learners would obviously enjoy working with a group or partner. However, they are also drawn to stories, real or fictional, and relate well to characters. Their acrostic sentences might read more as a narrative than as a definition.

Self-expressive learners like to think expansively and any of these types of acrostics would appeal to them. Of all the learning styles, self-expressive learners would probably find the most elegance in the modified acrostic whereas the mastery learners would find it too chaotic.

Creating Analogies

While students can solve analogies as a level two processing task, generating analogies requires an entirely different set of thought processes. One of the best documented structures for analogies is Shawn Glynn's Teaching-with-Analogies model (Glynn, 2007/2008; Paris & Glynn, 2004; Tate, 2016). Though originally studied as a teaching method that educators can use to explain complex science topics, it also serves as a handy tool for students to create their own analogies (Glynn, 2007).

While constructing analogies around target vocabulary words, students should keep in mind the limits of the analogies. Building analogies helps students take an active role in learning. It creates conceptual bridges between what is known and what they are trying to learn.

Rather than simple analogies, though, students should work to create elaborate analogies (Paris & Glynn, 2004). Elaborate analogies help students more accurately assess their own understanding of target terms. They provide students with personally relevant points of reference that enables them to evaluate their knowledge.

These analogies also serve as a self-diagnostic tool that fosters metacognitive thinking. They help create a mental framework for a word or concept and any related terms. Additionally, elaborate analogies increase students' sense of relevancy for the term or topic.

For students to create elaborate analogies, they must consider the vocabulary term and its characteristics. Words best suited for elaborate analogies are those that describe an action or a process. Target words, then, can be included in larger phrases or put into action to make them more accessible.

A previously-made semantic map, such as a concept of definition map (chapter 4) or a Frayer model (chapter 5), might help students fully examine the term. The goal is to find something similar to the target term that is familiar to the student. Students will utilize these two concepts to create the analogy.

First, students will identify the key features of the target word and the familiar concept. They will describe similarities between the two and show where the analogy breaks down (i.e., major differences). Finally, they will draw conclusions about any major ideas gleaned from comparing the word with the analogy.

Students can follow the six steps below to present their elaborate analogies (Glynn, 2007; Tate, 2016), either orally or in written form:

1. Introduce the word to be studied

2. Review a familiar concept that will serve in the analogy

3. Identify relevant features of the vocabulary word and the analog concept

4. Explain what both concepts have in common

5. Indicate differences that cause the analogy to break down

6. Draw conclusions about major ideas that other students should remember about the word

Heather finished creating her elaborate analogy and shared it with her table partner. "The word I am studying is joyously. It's an adverb used to describe when something is done with great happiness or excitement. It reminds me of hitting the game-winning shot in basketball. Both the word joyously and hitting the game-winning shot involve feelings of enjoyment. They aren't always the same, though. You can do something joyously without winning. Maybe you learn you passed your test or you got to see your favorite movie on opening night. You should remember that the word joyously can be used to describe when something happens that you feel super excited about, like hitting the game-winning shot."

Creating analogies involves multiple processes that lend themselves to the four major learning styles. The six steps described above will serve as a road map for mastery learners. They'll provide point-by-point instructions for successfully completing the task.

Understanding learners will enjoy exploring the similarities and differences between the word and the analog concept. They will probe deep in their examination of the related concepts and find hidden truths that other students might overlook.

Interpersonal learners, on the other hand, will find pleasure in choosing the analog concept for comparison. The ability to select something that is personally relevant to them will help them evaluate the target word more closely.

Finally, self-expressive learners will thrive with the fluid nature of this task. With the analog concept being open to choice and interpretation, they will make the most of their creativity.

Writing

A wonderful generative task for students to participate in is writing. While some students find it more enjoyable than others, writing is an excellent skill to develop in young learners. Writing is an essential part of the English language arts and, though it uses the same base language, writing requires a preciseness of intention not typically found when speaking.

Having a conversation with someone and writing that person a letter are two completely different uses of the English language (Nagy, 2007; Scott & Nagy, 2009). While the former utilizes facial cues, body language, tone, hand gestures, and a multitude of other non-verbal forms of communication, writing has none of those luxuries. One must rely on precise word choice and sentence structure to convey meaning when using written rather than spoken language. Thus a far richer vocabulary usually exists when students write down their thoughts.

In conversation, communication is largely dependent upon making use of shared beliefs, knowledge, and experiences (Scott & Nagy, 2009). On the other hand, written language typically does not have that shared context.

Authors cannot point to objects or use prosody (e.g., pitch, stress, and phrasing) to make themselves understood. Instead, word choice is often the most powerful tool at the disposal of writers.

Free Writing

One way to encourage students to write is to give them the option of free writing. As the name suggests, students choose to write about any topic they choose. They also choose the genre of writing, such as informational, fiction, personal letter, or memoir. The only requirement, then, is to use a certain amount of vocabulary words in their writing. Rather than dictating a certain number to use, students might respond better to the challenge of using as many words as possible.

Structured Writing

Some students might thrive with free writing while others might stare blankly at the paper for 45 minutes and claim they can't think of anything to write about. All it might take for certain students, then, is a few boundaries to start them on their path. Structure can take the form of suggestions about style of writing, topic, or audience.

Styles of writing include many different genres. Students can write about a favorite memory while including certain vocabulary words. They can write a summary of a topic or even the story the vocabulary words came from. Some might prefer to write a note to a friend while others might like to create an advertisement. With many genres to choose from, teacher- or student-selected writing styles will help focus some writers.

In addition, some children might be at a loss as to the topic they should write about. Sample topics include personal favorites, such as their favorite TV show, food, or hobby. Students could also write about a more general topic, such as friendship, courage, or honesty. Current events, directions for completing a task, and even opinions on topics of interest can serve to guide students in their writing.

Finally, writing changes based on the intended audience. A letter to a friend would involve different word choices than a letter to the principal. A newspaper editorial about the state of cafeteria food would look different than a diary entry on the same topic. Selecting a specific audience can also enhance students' writing.

However the writing is structured, the goal is to incorporate as many vocabulary words as possible. The writing should be evaluated primarily on two aspects. First, the usage of the vocabulary words should be rated. Were they used correctly? Does the context of the composition provide any support for the words' meanings? Second, the structure(s) put in place should be evaluated. Did the student write about the correct topic, use a style of writing effectively, and/or address the right audience?

Visual Writing

For students who are strong visual learners, another type of writing involves the use of a visual aid (Scott & Nagy, 2009). Rather than a verbal or written prompt, students could write in response to a picture. Images from the internet, a textbook, or even a picture book can serve as a boost to inspire young writers.

Quick writes can involve a simple picture and a short response to the image. Students can describe what is happening in the picture using vocabulary words. They might also write an imaginary conversation between people pictured in a photo. Additionally, they could write a brief descriptive story about how the situation in the picture came about.

Many wordless picture books exist, such as *Good Dog, Carl* by Alexandra Day, which could serve as a starting point for writing. Students could take a book and provide narration based on the pictures in the book. This task can conceivably be completed multiple times with the same book since the vocabulary words to be used would often change.

Mastery learners would most likely enjoy structured writing as a generative task. Given clear parameters and even a rubric for evaluating their work, these students could thrive in this type of open-ended task.

Understanding learners would be successful with any of the types of writing briefly mentioned. They would seek to showcase their grasp of the vocabulary words and any of these methods would provide them that opportunity.

Interpersonal learners would be drawn to the visual writing because of its potential for storytelling. Relating to the personal aspects of the images, they would cherish the chance to make the pictures come alive.

Lastly, the self-expressive learners would find free writing very appealing. Being given no boundaries or restrictions, they would greatly enjoy creating whimsical tales or exploring a wide range of topics. They can write poetry, songs, plays, captions, or even blog posts.

CHAPTER 8: PLAYING WITH WORDS

The final part of a powerful vocabulary program is word play. If words are always taken seriously, for the purpose of generating a grade or completing a worksheet, teachers run the risk of associating negative emotions to vocabulary instruction. Some students don't like work but they all like to play.

Keying in on creating a fun, word-friendly environment supports student motivation as well. One of the five facets of student motivation is emotions. By generating student interest and cultivating an exciting, risk-free, and playful atmosphere, teachers can engage students and increase word knowledge.

Benefits of Word Play

Word play should not be seen as something to do when the *real* work of vocabulary instruction is finished. Instead, it is a motivating and important component of a word-rich environment. Word play cannot be done passively but instead requires students to actively participate (Blachowicz & Fisher, 2004a; Blachowicz, Fisher, & Watts-Taffe, 2005). It requires students to reflect metacognitively on word parts and contexts (Blachowicz & Fisher, 2004a/2004b; Blachowicz, Fisher, & Watts-Taffe, 2005; Kelley, Lesaux, Kieffer, & Faller, 2010). Additionally, word play promotes curiosity in children as they develop an appreciation of word study (Anderson & Nagy, 1993; Kelley, Lesaux, Kieffer, & Faller, 2010).

Word play, as a component of a rich vocabulary program, develops word meanings in multiple domains. Designed to be done with others, it incorporates the motivational facet of relationships as it engages students in the practice and rehearsal of words. Within the larger descriptive category of word play lies many types of semantic manipulation, such as punning and joking. Overall, playing with words develops phonological, morphological, and syntactic awareness in students (Blachowicz & Fisher, 2004a).

Word Games

The rest of this chapter lines out some common games that students can play with words. Remember that though some of these activities look different than a traditional paper-and-pencil task, the level of thinking and reflection they require make them well worth students' time. Also, this is just a sampling of various ways to play with words and is not meant to be exhaustive. In fact, the only limits to the ways you can play with words is your imagination.

Charades

Many students will be familiar with the idea of charades, or acting out words, though the term itself might be unfamiliar. There are a few different ways that students can interact with words playing charades. In the traditional setup, students work together in small groups. One person acts out the word silently while the group tries to guess what is being represented. This can be done either competitively, where points are kept and teams battle against each other to guess the most words, or in a more relaxed manner.

Another form of this can be accessed quickly by the teacher using a whole-class approach. The teacher asks the students to stand next to their desks and act out words called out by the teacher. Rather than guessing what word is being demonstrated, the students hear the word and then try to show it with their actions. This will open up many possibilities for unique portrayals to start class conversations. Teachers should look for ideal or unique demonstrations and ask students for the rationale behind their creative choices (Blachowicz & Fisher, 2004a; Blachowicz, Fisher, & Watts-Taffe, 2005; Marzano & Pickering, 2005).

Draw Me

Similar to the popular game Pictionary, Draw Me asks students to visually represent words with original drawings. The customary way to play the game is similar to charades, in which small groups either work together or compete to guess what words are being drawn (Blachowicz & Fisher, 2004a; Blachowicz, Fisher, & Watts-Taffe, 2005; Marzano & Pickering, 2005).

Additionally, students can work in pairs to play Draw Me. Each pair would have a stack of vocabulary cards and each student would pick a card. At the same time, each partner would spend about one minute drawing their vocabulary word and then switch papers. After each student guesses what was drawn, the students talk briefly about why they drew what they did. It's the conversations that take place about vocabulary that have the greatest power to cement the words into long-term memory (Blachowicz & Fisher, 2004a; Blachowicz, Fisher, & Watts-Taffe, 2005).

Talk a Mile a Minute

This game requires students to use oral language and precision to describe words. In the game, one person from a pair or a small group is designated the Talker. The Talker has one minute to attempt to describe a list of words and have the other students guess as many as they can. When the first word has been guessed, the Talker moves on to the next word until the minute is up (Marzano & Pickering, 2005).

What makes this challenging is that the Talker cannot use the word itself or any rhyming words as clues. Instead, the Talker must define, describe, or use context to place the words in the mind of the other students. To make it more challenging, teachers can list a few synonyms next to the target words that may not be used, similar to the game Taboo (Blachowicz & Fisher, 2004a; Blachowicz, Fisher, & Watts-Taffe, 2005).

Card Games

Many different card games, such as those based on Go Fish, Old Maid, or Memory Match, emphasize the semantic relationships between words. Using a pairing principle, students work to find matches between vocabulary words and other related terms (Blachowicz & Fisher, 2004a).

The options for matching words are numerous. For a game such as Memory Match, students can work with a partner to pair up either vocabulary words with definitions or synonyms. For games that require sets of cards, sometimes called books, students can work to create a set of four cards: the vocabulary word, a synonym, a definition, and a symbol or picture.

Alternately, students can work together to match words with antonyms or finding matching cloze sentences. When using games that require more than one match to each vocabulary word, it would be wise to keep an answer key with the card games so disputes can be settled quickly. Students can even create many of these card games themselves.

Word Scrambles/Jumbles

Popular in newspapers for decades, Jumbles are simply words with their letters scrambled. The goal is for students to play with the letters, rearranging them until they form a recognizable word. Thus, an entire list of vocabulary words can be given to students at one time. Students can work together to unscramble the letters and find their vocabulary words (Blachowicz & Fisher, 2004a).

Looking at the example in Figure 18, some scrambled words from *The Ugly Duckling* (chapter 2) are displayed next to blank lines and circles. As the words are unscrambled and placed on the lines next to them, any letters placed in circles are used for the bonus word at the bottom, which is itself scrambled.

While this might seem simple to some, it will be laborious for others. One way to scaffold this form of word play would be to provide images or drawings next to each jumble. Students could use details from the pictures to help unscramble the words. Furthermore, a quick search of the internet using search terms like "create word scramble" will bring up many worksheet generating websites that will create the scrambles from words supplied by teachers.

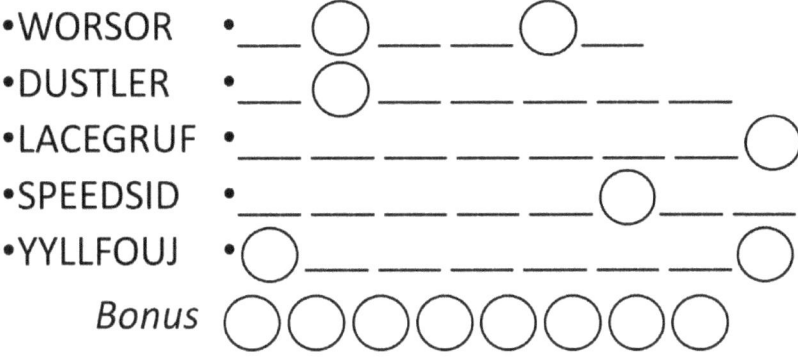

Figure 18: Word Scramble/Jumble

Synonym Strings

Students can also work together to build connected sets of synonyms. Conducted either with simple brainstorming or with the use of a thesaurus, students not only look for the relationships between words but also take note of the slight variations as the strings become longer.

Consider the example in Figure 19. The word *graceful* is being examined through the lens of a simple synonym string. As the words progress, they get more and more positive. One should also notice that the synonyms all relate to physical appearance rather than fluidity of motion. The object of the simple synonym string is to keep the synonyms closely related rather than meandering through gradients of meaning.

Synonym String

graceful
 beautiful
  charming
   attractive
    gorgeous

Figure 19: Simple Synonym String

More than one option is available for students when beginning a synonym string. For those wanting to compare divergent paths, they can create a dual synonym string like the one in Figure 20. This type of word play allows students to take disparate perspectives of word meanings and see how various permutations continue to alter the interpretations of the terms.

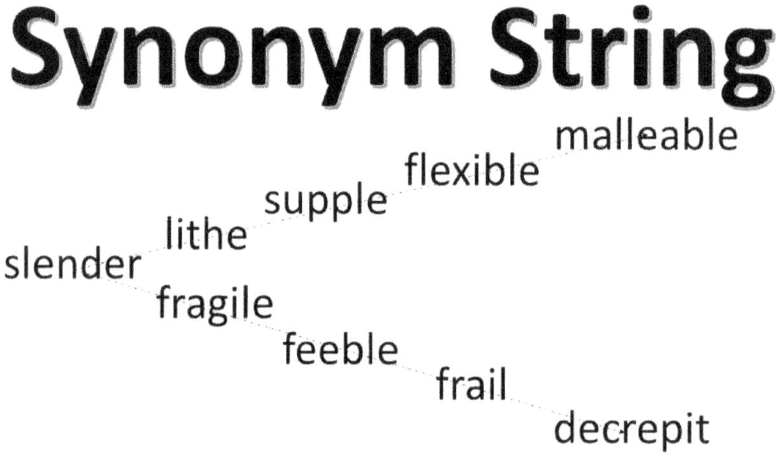

Synonym String

                              malleable
                       flexible
                 supple
           lithe
  slender
         fragile
            feeble
                frail
                   decrepit

Figure 20: Dual Synonym String

In Figure 20, two prominent synonyms are chosen for the original term *slender*. The top string, based off the synonym *lithe*, falls more in line with the original meaning in *The Ugly Duckling*. The bottom string, based off the synonym *fragile*, takes a more negative view of the starting term. As both strings are extended, students can see how far the two ending terms (i.e., *malleable* and *decrepit*) are from each other.

Finally, a third type of synonym string circles back on itself through many changes in meaning. Starting with the term *sorrow* and moving clockwise (Figure 21), synonyms meander from metaphorical descriptions to more physical words (e.g., agony, torture). At the word *pain*, the synonyms start to circle back on themselves and steer away from physical descriptions. The final term *unhappiness* itself is a synonym for *sorrow*, which completes the circular synonym string.

As students work together to create synonym strings, most likely with the help of a thesaurus, they should set out to create one of the specific types of strings. As the strings progress in difficulty, more and more care will have to be given when contemplating word choice. The circular synonym string in particular will take many attempts of trial and error before an adequate circle can be formed. By playing with the words as if they were puzzle pieces, students will come to appreciate the power of vocabulary.

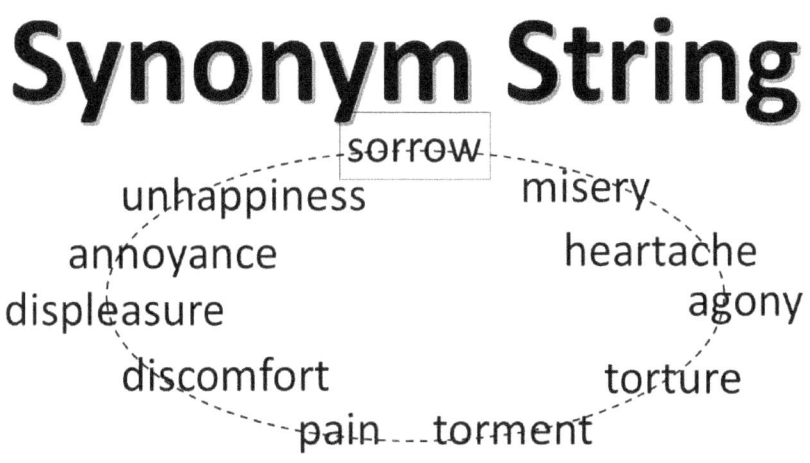

Figure 21: Circular Synonym String

In addition to creating synonym strings, students can also work together to dramatically present their strings to the class (Blachowicz & Fisher, 2004a). For example, after creating a circular synonym string like the one in Figure 21, students then create representations, like charades, of the various words. The goal is not to have students guess the words being demonstrated but to show slight variations as the connotations change.

Starting with *sorrow*, a student might say the word and then stand still with a sad, downcast face. Saying the next word, the student could begin to rub her eyes as if she were crying in *misery*. Moving on to *heartache*, the student could clutch her chest and look longingly into the distance. This continues until the demonstration returns to the original word.

Word Riddles

Word riddles are simple questions than have pun-like responses (Blachowicz & Fisher, 2004a). While they generally cause groans because of the over-the-top word manipulation of their questions and answers, students can create their own to demonstrate a deep and flexible use of language. One way to make word riddles is to choose a subject and generate a list of related terms. For example, if students are working with the subject of *pets*, some examples are *dog, cat,* and *hamster.*

Students then take the first letter off a related term (e.g., *cat*) and list words that begin with that letter cluster. Taking the *c* off *cat*, some words that start with *at-* are *atlas, attitude, attic,* and *athlete*. Then, putting the *c* back onto the new words, punny answers are created – *catlas, cattitude, cattic,* and *cathlete*. All that remains is to make up a riddle for the newly created terms.

Riddle: Where does a pet look when it wants to find maps of foreign countries?

Answer: In a catlas!

Riddle: How do you describe a feline that is always angry?

Answer: It has a bad cattitude!

Riddle: In which part of the house do pets love to play?

Answer: In the cattic!

Riddle: What do you call a pet that loves sports?

Answer: A cathlete!

Another type of word riddle students can create is based of rhyming patterns. Choosing a target word, such as *rustle* from *The Ugly Duckling*, students then list some words that rhyme with it (e.g., *bustle, hustle, muscle, tussle*). The goal is to create questions for which the answers will be the target word and a rhyming word paired together.

Riddle: What do you call it when someone moves quickly and makes soft noises?

Answer: A rustle bustle!

Riddle: What do you call it when you cheat someone in a quiet voice?

Answer: A rustle hustle!

Riddle: What do you call it when a bodybuilder in a tight-fitting nylon jacket flexes?

Answer: A muscle rustle!

Riddle: What do you call it when two brothers are quietly fighting?

Answer: A rustle tussle!

Categories

Remember that vocabulary words are taught not just to improve a student's lexicon but also to increase general knowledge. To that end, students can work alone or with a partner to fill in a simple grid based on a topic and a vocabulary word (Blachowicz & Fisher, 2004a; Blachowicz, Fisher, & Watts-Taffe, 2005).

Using the text from *The Ugly Duckling*, the teacher might want to focus on character emotions. Students could draw a simple grid with the rows containing the topics and the columns representing the starting letter for each box.

Categories

	G	R	A	C	E	F	U	L
Words that show happiness	glad				enjoy			lively
Words that show anger		rage	animosity	cross		fury		loathing
Words that show patience		relaxed		calm	endure	fortitude	unhurried	
Words that show shame	guilt	remorse	abashed		embarrass			

Figure 22: Categories

What is shown in Figure 22 is a sample of what students might come up with if working together to fill in the cells based on the clues in the first column and the letters of *graceful*. For this type of word play, it would be preferable for students not to use other resources such as a dictionary or thesaurus. Instead, they should pull from their own experiences and prior knowledge to complete the grid in the allotted time (e.g., three minutes).

Experienced teachers might foresee that this type of word play is open to many types of errors. What if students misapply a word? The culmination of this activity is a group discussion. Each team shares their words for each cell and the class, led by the teacher, evaluates and judges the worthiness of the words. If a group has a satisfactory word in a category that no other group could fill, they get 5 points. Otherwise, they get 3 points for categories filled by other groups if the words are unique and 2 points for categories that have a word repeated from another group.

The goal is not to compete, though that will surely motivate many students to get creative with their choice of words. Instead, the conversation about word selection and the justifications that students give are where the real learning takes place. For teachers that want to offer choice without creating competition, students could create their own tables and choose a word to place at the top. The categories in the first column would be the same but students could select a word (e.g., *despise, slender*) to use instead of every group using the same word.

Word Fluency

Word fluency asks students to generate as many synonyms or antonyms as possible within a given amount of time. This activity can either be accomplished individually or with a partner. Students can repeat this process multiple times and try to beat their previous scores (one point for each word).

Word Fluency

Word	Synonym
slender	slim
rustle	stir
persecute	struggle
sorrow	sadness
disagreeable	surly
despise	shun
graceful	supple
joyful	satisfied

Word	Antonym
slender	strong
rustle	silence
persecute	soothe
sorrow	satisfaction
disagreeable	sweet
despise	savor
graceful	stiff
joyful	sad

Figure 23: Word Fluency

Figure 23 shows various words from *The Ugly Duckling* in the first column and either synonyms or antonyms in the second column. The goal is list words that all start with the same letter (e.g., the letter *s*). While the example shows a completed example of both types, it would be better for students to begin with either synonyms or antonyms rather than both.

Regarding the letters to use for generating synonyms or antonyms, students should be directed to start with *s* as it is the most common initial letter in the English language. Following that, the next most common letters are *p*, *c*, *d*, *m*, and *a*. While it might be possible to use other letters with word fluency, it becomes increasingly difficult as the initial letters become less common.

Chapter 9: Putting the Parts Together

The five parts of a powerful vocabulary program work together to encourage students to wrestle with words. Instead of giving them static definitions to memorize within narrow contexts, true word learning is much deeper. When students embed newly learned words into complex semantic relationships, they begin to own their vocabulary.

Preparing is the first part of a powerful vocabulary program (chapter 2). Teachers analyze potential terms for both their usefulness and importance. When words have been prioritized and culled, teachers can then either assign them to students for study, ask students to rate their level of word knowledge to aid in selecting words, or a combination of the two.

Presenting the words through initial, direct instruction is an essential part of word learning (chapter 3). When considering what to include when sharing word meanings with students, teachers have many options to choose from. They can activate the students' prior knowledge or highlight any bases or affixes that make up various parts of the word. Some words are surrounded by ample context clues that can be used to help understand them. Descriptive definitions and examples also help assimilate new terms. Finally, synonyms, or friendly words, can shed light on the term while grammar usage offers additional word meaning clues.

Once students have been briefly introduced to the meanings of new terms, they should work on placing them into the context of their own experiences (chapter 4). Students can use a variety of semantic maps to connect vocabulary terms to their own prior knowledge. They can also engage in word association to aid in attaching unknown terms to a web of related ideas they already understand.

After a cursory interaction with the new terms, the fourth and largest part of a powerful vocabulary program is processing (chapters 5-7). Students should spend a significant amount of time making sense of the new terms with a multitude of processing tasks. Instead of one avenue of processing, though, students should work with words in a variety of learning styles (e.g., mastery, understanding, interpersonal, and self-expressive). Additionally, basic processing tasks ask students to comprehend new words while complex tasks require students to generate novel responses.

Finally, playing with words is the fifth part of a powerful vocabulary program (chapter 8). A plethora of games exist to allow students the opportunity to manipulate words in immensely enjoyable ways. Word play serves not only to boost student interest by generating positive emotions, it also is a great way to review previously learned terms to keep them fresh in students' minds.

Grading

Great instructional theory can sometimes get lost in the mundane aspects of teaching. Ideally no part of word study would be taken for a grade. Remember, it is the conversations, which are hard to quantify, and a safe (i.e., non-graded) environment that lead to a powerful vocabulary program. School policies and the expectations of principals, however, usually require a minimum number of grades each week. How can teachers maintain the spirit of wrestling with words and generate grades for their grade book at the same time?

Most classrooms already utilize a weekly or bi-monthly vocabulary test as a part of their normal routine. If this would meet school expectations, it can be used remain in compliance. One point to keep in mind, however, is that the true demonstration of word mastery comes from processing or play tasks, not selecting one right answer from four possibilities on a multiple-choice test.

If classwork grades also need to be generated, teachers can utilize vocabulary journals with their students. All of their thoughts and word work, from selecting words to playing with them can be documented in student journals. Students can then select one or two maps or processing tasks to turn in to be graded. Keeping these items as student-selected, rather than teacher-selected, helps promote autonomy and provides them with an opportunity for reflection as they choose their best pieces for evaluation. Alternately, teachers can collect journals periodically and simply grade for completion to keep students accountable.

Regardless of the grading requirements, the spirit of a powerful vocabulary program is not one of correctness but of wrestling with new words. The more this strays toward traditional grading, with activities given a number for percentage correct, the more that student thought becomes restricted. If their first aim is to seek the right answers rather than encoding the new terms into their existing semantic webs of knowledge, a great opportunity will be lost.

Scheduling

Another logistical matter to consider when contemplating the complexity of a powerful vocabulary program is scheduling. How can teachers of all subjects find the necessary time to encourage students to play with words without sacrificing time dedicated to core content instruction? Even this question is a bit misleading. Time spent on vocabulary instruction serves to bolster general instruction because well-chosen words encompass the main components of the content. Advancing word knowledge supports general learning.

Several scheduling options exist for carving out time for students to wrestle with words. While some advocate three minutes each day for five days a week (Blachowicz & Fisher, 2011), that small amount of time would restrict many students from diving deep. Instead of a simplistic formula, each teacher must make decisions based on his/her grade level and teaching schedule. If teachers can devote five to ten minutes a day for three or four days a week, that should be more than enough time for students to engage in vocabulary work without dominating the schedule.

Primary Grades

For teachers in primary grades, typically considered grades K-2, the use of centers is most likely already in place. Many language arts blocks include literacy centers, comprised of a variety of centers or stations for students to rotate through, including a word work station. This encompasses several components, ranging from learning the alphabet and letter sounds to grammar and vocabulary work. Depending on the level and instructional needs of the students, many parts of a powerful vocabulary program can be easily integrated into a word work station.

Centers sometimes extend beyond the language arts block. Many schools are moving toward working with stations in mathematics instruction. Since vocabulary words encompass knowledge, they can and should be wrestled with across all content areas. Mathematics especially is rich in content-specific terms that students must learn to gain greater computational dexterity.

A common method for math stations uses the acronym STACK, which stands for small groups, technology, apply, create, and kinesthetic. Even if a specific vocabulary station doesn't fit into the established rotation, many of the word play activities would work well in the kinesthetic station. Additionally, some processing tasks would fit nicely with the create station.

Sample Schedules

For teachers not in self-contained classrooms, time is of the essence. With some having as little as 45 minutes each day, carving out instructional time for wrestling with words can be daunting. The key principle to keep in mind when dealing with limited time is efficiency. How can teachers get the biggest bang for their buck without sacrificing precious minutes?

One solution would be to designate the first few minutes of each class to word work. Sometimes known as a bell ringer, teachers can maximize learning time by developing an entry routine for students. If students know that they have a learning task required of them from the time they come into the room, and if that task just happens to be fun, they'll be much more likely to come in and work right away. This will also help with tardiness since the activity will be designed to be brief but intense.

Proposed schedules will change based on how often a teacher wishes to engage in dedicated vocabulary work. Table 5 shows a variety of routines based on 3-day or 4-day schedules. Committing to a 5-day schedule is extremely difficult to maintain throughout the year. Friday is a great day to catch up on delays encountered throughout the week. Also, enough Monday or Friday holidays are scattered throughout the school year to drive the 5-day devotees nuts.

One part of a powerful vocabulary program, however, does not show up in the sample schedules in Table 5. Presenting new words should naturally exist within the flow of traditional teaching. As teachers encounter words through shared or guided reading, the best time to provide descriptive definitions or other parts of the ABCs of direct instruction is when the words are read or heard in their natural context. If students first encounter word meanings on their own without teacher guidance (e.g., during bell work), they sometimes lack have difficulty seeking additional clarification.

When considering a routine, teachers would be encouraged to periodically change things up. There is a distinct but sometimes invisible line between consistency and falling into a rut. Even the most engaging vocabulary strategies will lose their potency if followed religiously for 30 straight weeks.

Implementation should begin with teacher-directed activities in each of the areas until students gain flexibility with each component. As students repeatedly work with a particular facet, such as drawing semantic maps or playing charades, teachers can begin to provide students with choices. If they have worked with several strategies within a part of the vocabulary program, they can eventually choose how they want to play or process their vocabulary words for that week.

Table 5: Sample Schedules

	Monday	Tuesday	Wednesday	Thursday
3-day (1)		Prepare (student choice)	Place	Process (basic or complex)
3-day (2)		Place	Process (basic)	Process (complex)
3-day (3)		Place	Process (basic or complex)	Play
4-day (1)	Prepare (student choice)	Place	Process (basic or complex)	Play
4-day (2)	Place	Process (basic)	Process (complex)	Play

APPENDIX 1: VOCABULARY SELECTION

Several researchers and literacy experts have, in their work with vocabulary individually and as a larger part of language development, have addressed the issue of how to choose the best vocabulary words for instruction. Operating off the supposition that some words have more value than others, how can teachers be assured that their precious instructional minutes are not spent teaching obscure or overly familiar words?

Word Classifications

First, teachers should be familiar with several different ways that words have been classified by type, usefulness, and immediacy. One method sorts words into various types based on their relationship to the text (Blachowicz, Fisher, & Watts-Taffe, 2005). These categories are comprehension words, useful words, academic words or phrases, and generative words. All four of these word types are suggested for instruction as long as they are not previously known words or explicitly explained in the text.

Comprehension words are deemed essential to understanding the selection and/or critical to the overall unit of study. Useful words, then, are not as critical to the particular domain being considered but are likely to be encountered in other contexts. Academic words or phrases can potentially cause trouble for students with language or academic deficiencies. Finally, generative words introduce further word study or strategy instruction (e.g., affixes, root words).

Additionally, Michael Graves and colleagues (Graves, 2016; Graves, Baumann, & Blachowicz, 2014) propose a four-part classification method called Selecting Words for Instruction from Text (SWIT). The SWIT method also classifies words into various types to separate their uses, assuming of course that they are unfamiliar to the students. These four types are essential words, valuable words, accessible words, and imported words.

Essential words are crucial for comprehending the text under consideration. In narrative texts, these words often relate to understanding the central story elements, the characters, and their actions. Valuable words are generally useful for both reading and writing across multiple contents. Not determined directly by their relation to the selection, these words increase the vocabulary sophistication of students.

In addition, accessible words include more common or higher frequency words that are not likely to be understood by students with limited vocabulary experience. Though known by the majority of students, these words will trip up struggling students and hinder comprehension. Finally, imported words are not included in the text but enhance a reader's understanding or learning from a text. These words might capture thematic elements while not being used explicitly.

Another method used to sort words based on usefulness for instruction is the tier method developed by Isabel Beck and her colleagues (Beck, McKeown, Wagner, Muse, & Tannenbaum, 2007). Tier 1 words consist of the most basic words. Since children entering school are typically familiar with these words, direct instruction is most likely not needed with these words. Tier 3 words, on the other hand, consist of words whose frequency of use is quite low or whose use is restricted to a specific domain.

Tier 2 words, in contrast, are seen as the most useful and should be the focus of instructional efforts (Graves, Baumann, & Blachowicz, 2014). Due to their high frequency and general utility, they deserve the most attention by teachers. Rich knowledge of these words can have a significant impact on the verbal functioning of students (Beck, McKeown, Wagner, Muse, & Tannenbaum, 2007). They include not only words essential to understanding a selection but also include academic vocabulary used across the curriculum (Brief, 2008).

Additionally, words can be classified by their place in the instructional cycle. Flanigan and Greenwood (2007) suggest a 4-level framework for evaluating which words to teach. Level 1 words are critical "before" words that are absolutely essential to understanding the passage. They represent concepts that students need an in-depth understanding of before reading. Without this instruction, students will find it difficult to navigate the passage and construct meaning.

Level 2 words are considered "foot-in-the-door" words which, like Level 1 words, are critical to understanding the text. The difference, however, is that students only need a basic understanding of these words to understand the gist of the passage. They require only a short amount of instructional time and consist of two subtypes. New label/new concept words represent unfamiliar concepts and can typically be taught by providing a clear definition and a rich sentence with contextual clues. New words/familiar concepts, on the other hand, can be addressed simply by providing the definition or a synonym since the underlying idea is familiar to students.

Level 3 words, or critical "after" words, represent concepts that are important for the students to know on some level but are not necessary to understand the reading selection. They can be dealt with either during the reading or afterwards. Level 3 words normally fall into four categories. They can be content words that don't interfere with text comprehension, those that are clearly defined in the text, high-utility words that will most likely be seen in other settings, or words that can be used to teach preciseness of language, (e.g. *wolf down* instead of *eat*).

Finally, just as important as knowing what to teach is knowing what to ignore. Level 4 words represent just that – words not to teach. These words have many characteristics, including already known words, words that do not serve instructional goals, and words that can be understood using rich contextual clues.

4-Quadrant Vocabulary

When reviewing the weight of literacy and vocabulary research, two common themes emerge about selecting which words to teach. Educators should focus their energy on words that are highly important and highly useful. Rather than treating all words equally, teachers can best leverage instructional minutes by choosing the terms that can do the most good in the least amount of time.

Important words are those that would fall into Beck's second tier (Beck, McKeown, Wagner, Muse, & Tannenbaum, 2007; Beck & McKeown, 1991; Blachowicz, Fisher, & Watts-Taffe, 2005; Brief, 2008; Flanigan & Greenwood, 2007; Graves, 2016; Graves, Baumann, & Blachowicz, 2014; Nagy & Townsend, 2012). They are essential to understanding the text or unit of study. Without a firm understanding of these words, comprehension will be hampered or even stopped altogether. Important words tend to remain focused on the topic under consideration.

Useful words, on the other hand, have a much broader appeal. Though related to the text being examined, they also have value across the contents (Beck & McKeown, 1991; Beck, McKeown, Wagner, Muse, & Tannenbaum, 2007; Blachowicz, Fisher, & Watts-Taffe, 2005; Brief, 2008; Graves, 2016; Graves, Baumann, & Blachowicz, 2014; Kelley,

Lesaux, Kieffer, & Faller, 2010). These terms are frequently seen in multiple subjects in a variety of contexts. When useful words are selected for instruction, student knowledge increases far beyond the current unit of study.

To visually represent these two factors when choosing the best words to study, I created a continuum called 4-Quadrant Vocabulary (Figure 24). By placing word importance along the vertical axis and word usefulness along the horizontal axis, teachers can quickly evaluate the priority of words under consideration. Unlike the four quadrants of the coordinate plane in mathematics, the quadrants in 4-Quadrant Vocabulary are numbered in order of their instructional importance.

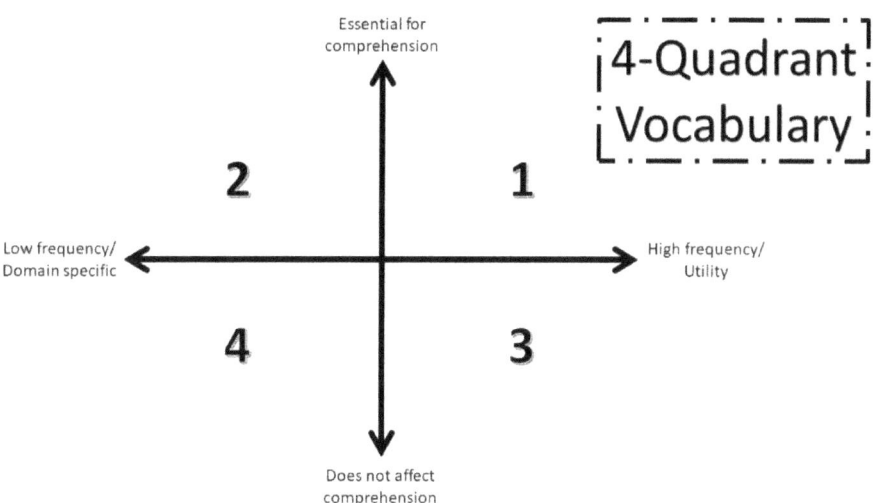

Figure 24: 4-Quadrant Vocabulary

The first quadrant contains words that rank high in both importance and usefulness. With value for the present reading selection or unit of study and for broad, general knowledge as well, these words are pedagogical gold mines. If only a few words fall in this category and others must also be included for instruction, the choice falls to words that are either high in importance but low in usefulness or vice versa. Between the two, teachers should consider words that are necessary for text comprehension (quadrant two). Since the study of vocabulary is most likely related to new learning being undertaken, comprehension of the main points of that content is essential.

Though not necessarily essential for understanding the text, selecting words in the third quadrant allows teachers to broaden the overall vocabulary of their students. The benefits of these words might not be seen immediately but will cumulatively increase the language proficiency of students.

Finally, some words simply don't need to be taught. If they are specific to the particular domain (not useful) and ignorance of their meaning will not jeopardize comprehension (not important), time is better spent elsewhere. Teachers should ignore these quadrant four words and focus most of their attention on first- and second-quadrant words.

Questions to Help Select Vocabulary

Once the decision has been made to focus on first quadrant words that are both important and useful, how are those words identified? At this point teachers must use their judgment and experience to evaluate and rank words based on those two criteria. There are, however, some questions that can be asked to help the process along.

One set of queries (Brief, 2008) seeks to classify words by usefulness and relatedness. Teachers can ask themselves the following questions to identify the best words to teach.

> How useful is the word? Are students likely to encounter it often in other texts? Will it be of use to students in describing their own experiences?

> How does the word relate to other words or ideas that students know or have been learning? Does it directly relate to a topic of study in the classroom? Will it add a dimension to the ideas that have been developed?

What does the word bring to a text or situation? What role does it play in communicating the meaning of the context in which it is used?

Similarly, Blachowicz and colleagues (Blachowicz, Fisher, & Watts-Taffe, 2005) suggest investigating the importance, usefulness, and necessity of spending time teaching the words under consideration. The following questions can be helpful when choosing which words to teach.

How important is the word to the reading selection or unit of study?

How useful is the word outside of the selection or theme?

Is this a word that students might learn independently, perhaps through context?

Is this a word that will heighten students' enthusiasm for word learning?

Finally, teachers might use a decision-making model to evaluate which words to directly teach (Fisher, Frey, & Hattie, 2016). First teachers would question how representative the word is using questions like the following.

Is the word representative of a family of words the student will need to know?

Is the word or phrase representative of a concept the student will need to know?).

If that condition is met, teachers then examine the transportability of the word by asking if the word or phrase will be needed in discussion, reading, and/or writing tasks. If a word is both representative and transportable, teachers then decide how the word knowledge will be acquired.

One option is merely through word frequency. For example, if the word appears frequently in the text, direct instruction might not be needed. Another method is to use contextual analysis to determine if the word or phrase presents an opportunity for the student to apply contextual analysis skills to resolve word meaning. Also, structural analysis of the word itself (e.g., affixes, roots) can be used to learn the meaning of the word.

If none of these choices seem viable (i.e., word frequency, contextual analysis, structural analysis), direct instruction of the word would be appropriate. However, if word meaning can be attained through one of those three methods, students should do so and instructional time should be reserved for other needed words.

Collating the various sets of questions, then, should be done with a view of the two dimensions of importance and usefulness in 4-Quadrant Vocabulary. Using Table 1 (chapter 2), teachers can use the following questions to evaluate words for instruction. To use the table, teachers can simply ask each question of the word under consideration and answer either yes or no. The more questions that can be answered positively, the more important or useful the word is.

Another way to use the questions is to chart them using 4-Quadrant Vocabulary with Scales. Like plotting a coordinate pair in mathematics, successive positive answers to questions of usefulness can be plotted on the x-axis. Likewise, the number of positive answers to questions of importance will determine how high the word is graphed on the y-axis (see Figure 1 in chapter 2).

For example, a teacher might be considering two words to include within a vocabulary lesson but only has time for direct instruction on one word. If the first word has two positive answers to usefulness questions and five positive answers to importance questions, this would place it in the second quadrant. The other word might have three positive answers to both sets of questions. This would place it in the first quadrant and prioritize it over the first word.

Word Knowledge

Alongside various methods using to sort words for instruction, another avenue involves considering students' familiarity or knowledge of the words under consideration. For example, students might rate words in one of three ways – can define it/use it, heard it, and don't know (Blachowicz, Fisher, & Watts-Taffe, 2005; Phillips, Foote, & Harper, 2008).

Others recommend using a four-level sorting of word knowledge (Blachowicz, Fisher, & Watts-Taffe, 2005; Brief, 2008). Level 1 words are unknown and students can say, "I have never heard that word before." Level 2 words represent limited knowledge that the word exists about which students can say, "I've heard that word before." Level 3 words are partially known and when considering them, students think, "I have a general understanding of the word." Finally, level 4 words are completely known and students can define the word and use it correctly.

In the same strain, word knowledge can be classified in four stages (Beck & McKeown, 1991; Pythian-Sence & Wagner, 2007). Rather than being an all-or-nothing proposal, understanding of a word can be viewed in degrees. Stage 1 words have never been seen by the students while stage 2 words have been heard before but their meaning is not known. Stage 3 words can be recognized when viewed in context while stage 4 words are known well.

Others consider a five-part continuum of word knowledge (Graves, 2016; Pythian-Sence & Wagner, 2007). At one end of the continuum is words that have never been seen before and words that have been heard but are still unknown. In the middle of the continuum is a narrow, context-bound knowledge. On the other end of the spectrum is knowledge without the ability to recall the word readily and finally a rich, decontextualized knowledge.

Synthesizing the various approaches to levels of word knowledge, I suggest that students use a simple, four level scale to rate their level of word knowledge (Figure 2 in chapter 2). They can give each potential word a value of one to four based on how familiar they are with the word. The difference between level 3 knowledge ("I know it") and level 4 knowledge ("I own it") is the degree to which students feel comfortable using the word outside of the present context in self-generated conversation or writing. Owning a word is more than simply being able to recite a definition. Instead, this level of word knowledge gives students the flexibility to use the word in unique situations at a moment's notice.

In considering the many frameworks that exist to select appropriate words for vocabulary instruction, most agree that the focus should be in high-utility academic words (Beck & McKeown, 1991; Kelley, Lesaux, Kieffer, & Faller, 2010; Nagy & Townsend, 2012). In addition to teacher-selected words, having students identify words to study connects them more closely with the vocabulary (Phillips, Foote, & Harper, 2008) and builds motivation and study skills (Blachowicz C. L., Fisher, Ogle, & Watts-Taffe, 2006).

APPENDIX 2: DIRECT VOCABULARY INSTRUCTION

Words are labels for concepts. When you read the word *lemon*, you should instantly think of a yellow citrus fruit. If you've had a bad car-buying experience, you might relate the word *lemon* to a lousy vehicle, but for the most part everyone can agree on what a lemon is.

If I were to teach this word to someone who didn't know what a *lemon* was, my goal would be to help them understand the underlying concept of a lemon. I could give them a technical explanation, such as:

Noun: the yellowish, acid fruit of a subtropical citrus tree

But does that really convey what a lemon is? Can someone truly understand what a lemon is by simply reciting a dictionary definition? How can one understand the concept of *lemon* without having some experience with it through one of the five senses? Tasting its sour juices, feeling the rough rind, smelling the sweet aroma, or seeing the stark yellowness would greatly help someone truly know what a lemon was.

To know a word, you must be equipped with more than a glossary definition (Anderson & Nagy, 1993). The difference between rank three (i.e., I know it) and rank four (i.e., I own it) on the Word Knowledge Scale (Figure 2 in chapter 2) revolves around the depth and flexibility of understanding.

When students can use a word in multiple contexts and differentiate between shades of meaning, they begin to own the word.

Teachers should keep in mind that the aim of vocabulary instruction is to help students reach a rank four knowledge of the word. That in itself entails much more than a simple dictionary definition. When the knowledge behind a word is the goal, retention is greatly improved. The aim is not to improve SAT scores or help students on an assessment. Instead, vocabulary words, like all words, represent a concept and the goal is to increase conceptual knowledge (Nagy & Herman, 1984).

Elements of Direct Instruction

To teach a word such as *lemon*, students would need varied experiences with the word to begin to learn it. Solid instructional practices include definitional, contextual, and usage information. Teachers should also employ examples and non-examples, synonyms and descriptions, and activate prior knowledge when applicable.

Descriptive Definitions

The general consensus among literacy experts and researchers is that the most effective vocabulary instruction includes both definitional and contextual information about the word (Blachowicz & Fisher, 2004; Blachowicz, Fisher, & Watts-Taffe, 2005; Blachowicz, Fisher, Ogle, & Watts-Taffe, 2006; Graves, 2015; Graves, Baumann, & Blachowicz, 2014; Mebarki, 2011; Nagy, 1988; Nagy & Townsend, 2012; Pythian-Sence & Wagner, 2007; Stahl & Fairbanks, 1986). In addition, some advocate that grammar usage information should also be expressed when teaching new vocabulary words (Blachowicz & Fisher, 2004b; Blachowicz, Fisher, & Watts-Taffe, 2005).

While definitional information about a word is vital, that information in isolation does not have a lasting effect on vocabulary acquisition (Anderson & Nagy, 1993; Blachowicz, Fisher, Ogle, & Watts-Taffe, 2006; Marzano, 2009; Stahl & Fairbanks, 1986). Definitional information involves the knowledge of relationships between the word and other known words (Stahl & Fairbanks,

1986). When teaching *lemon*, words that relate it to the concept of fruit, specifically citrus fruit, will help define it. Additionally, the fact that it grows on trees will also aid in learning the word.

While the starting place for vocabulary instruction is providing a definition, it should be done so with an informal description or explanation of the term (Beck, McKeown, Wagner, Muse, & Tannenbaum, 2007; Marzano & Pickering, 2005). If you were to try and teach a friend about a lemon, your first instinct would not be to describe it as a yellowish, acid fruit of a subtropical citrus tree. Instead, you would most likely use a more descriptive, conversational method to share your knowledge.

"A lemon is a type of fruit but it's not sweet like a pear or an apple. Instead, it has a rough outer rind and has a sour taste. It's small, yellow, and grows on trees. It's used as an ingredient in some cleaning liquids and, when combined with a lot of sugar, makes a sweet drink called lemonade."

Our natural inclination when explaining an unknown concept is to define it but also to place it in context with examples. Our understanding of a lemon goes far beyond a dictionary definition. That should also be the goal of classroom vocabulary instruction. When focusing on conceptual knowledge rather than a recitation of bland phrases, defining a word requires depth and intentionality.

Contextual Information

Contextual information, on the other hand, refers to the text or passage in which the word is found. Words do not operate in isolation but work together to paint a picture of meaning. When using direct instruction to teach words, both a conversational definition and information as to how the word fits into the surrounding context should be included.

Presenting words in context rather than in isolation greatly helps understanding and is more naturalistic. If the words can be reinforced in new contexts as well, word knowledge increases (Blachowicz, Fisher, & Watts-

Taffe, 2005). All contexts do not supply sufficient support for defining new words, however. Teachers should examine the sentences and paragraphs surrounding a vocabulary word before instruction.

"Let's look at our vocabulary word *lemon*. I have two sentences from the short story that use the word for us to examine. The first sentence says, 'The lemon is really grown upon a bitter orange tree, grafted to bear a lemon.' From this sentence I can tell that a lemon is a part of something alive because it is grown. It has something to do with fruit because it's grown on a bitter orange tree. Perhaps it's closely related to an orange because it's grafted, or transplanted, onto an orange tree.

"The other sentence from the selection comes from a conversation between Martha and her mother. Her mother says, 'If you want to get a red-based stain out, you have to use lemon, dish soap and hot water.' In addition to being something grown on a tree, this sentence lets me know that lemons are used in cleaning. This makes me think the juice from a lemon, rather than the lemon itself, is helpful in removing stains. I know that orange juice is something that people can drink so most likely lemons produce a juice as well."

So much of our understanding of a word comes from the context in which it is read or heard. The first sentence describes a lemon as a fruit grown from a tree. This is most likely representative of the first thing that come to mind when thinking about a lemon. However, a lemon is much more than a citrus fruit. As evidenced by the second sentence, lemon is a cleaning agent. By providing contextual as well as definitional information about a word, students will begin to have a more solid understanding of the term under consideration.

Grammar Usage

Sometimes how words are used in context can be illuminated to increase knowledge. By providing multiple types of information about each word, students can begin to gain a more robust understanding of each word

(Blachowicz, Fisher, Ogle, & Watts-Taffe, 2006). These can include affixes, roots, and even word origins.

For example, students might come across the term *lemony cookie*. This provides an opportunity to discuss how the addition of the suffix *-y* to the root word *lemon* changes it from a noun to an adjective. Instead of referring to a lemon itself, *lemony* modifies or adds to the meaning of the noun (cookie). Rather than it being a normal cookie, they can determine that is has a lemon flavor.

Sometimes word origins also help define a word. Students might be interested to know that lemon comes from the Old French word *limon* which in modern French refers to a lime. Sometimes the term *lemon-lime* is used when describing a flavor and students should know that both are citrus fruits whose main difference is their size (lemons are larger), color (limes are green), and flavor (limes are more bitter while lemons are more sour).

Instead of focusing on a simple word like *lemon*, students should build a large conceptual framework around the word and various ways it is used. This not only builds understanding but will help them in future readings if they come across similar words with the same root, such as *lemonish* or *lemonlike*.

Examples and Non-Examples

In addition to providing an informal definition and any contextual clues that might exist, word knowledge can be enhanced by providing examples and non-examples of the word (Graves & Fitzgerald, 2006; Marzano & Pickering, 2005; Nagy, 1988). How we define a word sometimes has as much to do with what it isn't as what it is. This is especially true when dealing with words that have connotational significance when compared to other words.

Take the word *minute* for example. Devoid of context, this word can have vastly different definitions. While most might think about a unit of time equal to sixty seconds, I could be referring to the definition that has to do with size. A good sentence to help define this would be, "He closely examined the minute particles with a microscope." In that context, students would see that it is used as an adjective, rather than a noun, to describe how small something is.

To drive home the point, teachers can provide examples and non-examples of relatable information to help solidify the meaning of the term.

> "Let's look at the word *minute*. It's an adjective that describes something that is extremely small. An ant is minute but a puppy isn't. A cell is minute but a fingernail isn't. Also, a dust mite is minute but a pencil is only small."

By taking a word and comparing it to other known concepts, it helps embed the idea in relation to what is already understood. Students might not at first grasp the nuances of the word *minute* but can better grasp it when contrasting minute things (e.g., ant, cell, dust mite) with small things (e.g., puppy, fingernail, pencil). The more connections teachers can make to a new word, either by comparison or by contrast, the closer students get to owning the word.

Prior Knowledge

A result of descriptive definitions, examples and non-examples, and possibly even contextual information is the activation of prior knowledge. Utilizing prior knowledge is not only a hallmark of good vocabulary instruction (Nagy, 1988; Nagy & Herman, 1984; Scott & Nagy, 2009), it also meshes with what is known about brain-based teaching strategies (Willis, 2006).

Imagine that as a small child you were handed ten index cards which each had a word written on it: puppy, zebra, goat, dinosaur, egg, feather, fly, roach, milk, and giraffe. Now consider your mind as filled with small cubbies with various labels. If you had been handed the index cards and told to put them in the correct cubbies in your mind, you might not have enough information to place them in the correct spot.

Activating prior knowledge helps the mind decide where to store the information and what it relates to. If you don't know what a zebra is but you were shown a picture of one, you might note that it looks similar to a horse and file the word *zebra* in the horse-like cubby along with horse, pony, and donkey. Likewise, you might not know where to put *roach* but if I describe it as a type of bug or insect, you could then relate it to other bugs you knew of. Teaching the whole before the part helps students place words in the proper context (Jenson, 2005; Willis, 2006).

Relating new words to concepts that are already known builds connections that increase learning. These relationships also help memory recall. When students need to later use the new word to aid in comprehension, they will have an easier time remembering its meaning if it's properly labeled with other known words. To extend the metaphor, trying to remember a word that isn't tied to anything previously known is akin to trying to find a word in a dictionary if the words in the dictionary were not listed in alphabetical order.

Synonyms

Finally, another method that can be used to provide initial direct instruction is to provide synonyms for the new word (Graves, Baumann, & Blachowicz, 2014). Sometimes known as "friendly words" in the primary grades, synonyms provide a starting point for some students if the concept is known but the new word or label is not (Nagy, 1988; Scott & Nagy, 2009).

For the word *minute*, simply giving examples or non-examples might not be enough. It would be difficult to visually represent something that is minute because it would be very hard to see. However, students can explore friendly words that are either synonyms or somehow related to the target word.

> "One of our words to study this week is *minute*. It refers to something that is really tiny. Yet it means so much more than just very small. A synonym for *minute* is *microscopic*. You might not know the word *microscopic* but you can see that it's related to the word

microscope.

"Microscopes are used to see things that can't be seen with the naked eye. If something is microscopic, then, that means it is so small that it can't be seen without the help of powerful lenses. In the same way, when something is described as *minute*, it usually means it is extremely small or insignificant."

Direct Instruction: ABCDEFG

So which components are most important when using direct instruction to teach students new vocabulary words? How can teachers best navigate all the aforementioned strategies without devoting fifteen minutes of instructional time to each word? The key is understanding that there is no pedagogical silver bullet. No single method of vocabulary instruction has been found to be superior to others. Successful teaching incorporates a variety of techniques and repeated exposures (Beck & McKeown, 1991).

Putting all the methods together into an acrostic, teachers can use the first seven letters of the alphabet to remember the various ways to directly teach vocabulary words. Taken in roughly the order shown in Figure 3 (chapter 3), these seven strategies represent a solid instructional cycle for vocabulary instruction. Individually, though, teachers should employ several methods when engaging in vocabulary instruction. Rather than just sharing a definition or looking at context clues for each word, teachers can treat the ABCs of direct vocabulary instruction as a menu to choose from when discussing new words.

The more varied the initial instruction, the more relationships the students will build between new words and existing knowledge. Instead of seeing unfamiliar terms in isolated contexts, they should explore its nuances in a variety of settings. By using descriptive definitions, friendly synonyms, and examples and non-examples, among others, initial vocabulary instruction can be rich and multifaceted.

APPENDIX 3: MEMORY AND MOTIVATION

Quality vocabulary instruction, in addition to finding a solid footing in literacy research, also incorporates more general principles. With all that is known about how memories are formed, teachers can design their instruction to maximize neural connections. In addition, over 30 years of educational and psychological research has detailed the various factors that influence student motivation. Both of these components will be briefly discussed in this appendix and their implications are woven throughout the remainder of this book. Wrestling with words isn't just fun – it substantially increases student engagement and retention of knowledge.

Memory

One of the many goals of instruction is for students to remember the learned information after the lesson is over. While cramming for a test might result in a passing grade, it will most likely not have a lasting impact on the student. Most of us have had the experience of meeting someone new and then immediately forgetting his/her name within five seconds of hearing it. What causes some things to be remembered decades after the memory was initially formed and other things to be forgotten almost immediately?

When teachers engage students in learning, the brain receives input from the five senses, emotions, and/or internally-generated stimuli (e.g., imagination, reflection). The input is shunted over to working memory and can only stay there for a limited amount of time. To keep the information from slipping away, something needs to be done with the input. It needs to be encoded into the larger network of the brain's wiring or risk being lost forever (Willis, 2006).

There are many ways for teachers to help students encode new information into long-term memory. The strategies presented in this book are designed specifically to harness the brain's natural methods of making memories. The goal of vocabulary instruction, like all instruction, is to provide ready knowledge that can be accessed and used flexibly when needed.

Constructing Knowledge

The first thing one should know about how our brains work is that learning in general is based in activity, not reception. We are constantly constructing knowledge, and rewiring our brains in the process, by interacting with our world. Experiences sculpt our neurons, synapses, and overall brain activity. On the other hand, simply being exposed to events and information has little lasting impact on our brains (Fischer, 2009).

Teaching, then, should be based on interactive experiences rather than lectures. Since memorable learning requires active construction of knowledge, students should be hard at work throughout the school day on meaningful tasks. Administrators should not walk into a classroom and find that the hardest working person in the room is the teacher. It's the students, not the teacher, who must do the learning. Thus it is the students that should shoulder the mental load of thinking.

Consider how you learn to do anything well. Whether it be playing a guitar or juggling, reading about and/or watching demonstrations will only take you so far. To really understand something, you must interact with it. In the words of a famous shoe and apparel company, "Just Do It!"

Activating Prior Knowledge

One method to help students actively construct knowledge is to have them relate their previous experiences with the new information. For example, teachers can ask students to connect the learning with something they learned earlier in the year. By activating prior knowledge, students work to recognize patterns between new and current information. It is these connections that help the new data travel into the brain's long-term storage areas (Willis, 2006).

Imagine that your brain is a multi-faceted filing system that serves to store information and also act as a resource for interpreting current experiences. As you are constantly bombarded by sensory information every second of every day, your brain has to filter the important from nonessential input. Some information is tagged and filed away while the vast majority is discarded instantly. In the midst of all of the stimuli competing for attention, teachers attempt to instruct students in new concepts every day.

Activating prior knowledge, then, helps encode the new information with a retrieval-friendly tag. Rather than simply one more item that might not ever make it out of working memory, connecting new learning with prior knowledge helps immensely. Current memories already have brain space devoted to them and attaching new learning to them gives them a ready location to be filed and stored. The stronger the prior knowledge, the easier it will be to later recover the newly connected learning.

When students can relate new knowledge to something they already know, they expand their mental maps to include the new information. By fitting the new items into patterns already encoded into memory, the brain greatly increases the chances of those new memories being recalled later. Education, then, would do well to increase the patterns that students can use, recognize, and communicate in order to acquire additional knowledge. Tying learning into existing relationships generates greater brain cell activity and achieves more successful memory storage and retrieval capability (Willis, 2006).

Repeated Exposures

In addition to activating prior knowledge, one of the most powerful practices described in brain-based learning research is the strategic use of repeated exposures in memory creation. After multiple experiences with an idea, working memories begin to coalesce as neuronal circuits, ready to be activated when the information is needed again. When a memory has been recalled often, the associated brain matter becomes more and more developed because of its repeated activation and use (Willis, 2006).

Thinking of the brain as muscle, one can begin to see how repeated exposures build stronger memories. Just as targeting certain muscle groups with regular weight training will result in a buildup of muscle mass, neural connections become more efficient and easier to access with practice. For better or worse (depending on your habits), neurons that fire together, wire together!

A simple way to explain this to students would be to take a short walk outside. Walk through a grassy area in single file and then look back on the path you took. Ask students if they can see a trail marked by their passing feet. The students will probably notice the grass flattened a bit and could retrace their steps if needed. Then tell them that what they are seeing is like working memory. It can keep something only for a little while before disappearing.

Bring the class back out the next day and ask them if they can find their trail. The evidence of their passing will have disappeared and they would have to start over again. At this point the teacher can ask them a hypothetical question. "I know that we walked a path yesterday but we can't find it today. What do you think would happen if we walked the same path every day for 10 days? 50 days? 100 days?"

Students should picture a trail beginning to emerge because of regular use. By the 100th day, the grass itself might be worn down to bare earth. This, then, is similar to how learning can be strengthened.

Repeated exposures to content will result in more noticeable neural pathways and make the content easier to remember when called upon.

Multiple Pathways

If simply doing something repeatedly was sufficient, drill-and-kill worksheets would be a valid teaching tool. The problem with rote memorization, however, is that what is learned through this method usually holds little interest for the student. If the material lacks emotional value as well, it will be stored in more remote areas of the brain. These isolated facts will be difficult to locate later because of the relatively few connections (Willis, 2006).

The key, then, is to tie the information to as many neural pathways as possible. The more pathways that connect to the learned information, the easier it will be for students to retrieve it for use later. In general, memories are classified in two broad categories – explicit and implicit (Jenson, 2005).

Explicit memories are divided into two subsections – semantic and episodic. Sematic memories deal with words, symbols, abstractions, videos, and textbooks, among other things (Jenson, 2005). As you read this page at this very moment, it is being filtered through your brain as a semantic memory. Unfortunately, unless something is done to strengthen the memory you are creating right now, it will vanish shortly.

The other type of explicit memory is episodic. These memories are tied to locations, events, and circumstances (Jenson, 2005). Where are you right now? Are you in a memorable location or somewhere mundane? If you were to read this chapter while meditating at the top of Half Dome in Yosemite National Park, it would most likely be unforgettable.

This is because the more ways something is learned, the more memory pathways there are to connect to it. More stimulations result in a better memory. When multiple regions of the brain store data about a memory (e.g., semantic, episodic), the interconnectivity increases. This redundancy helps recall because various memory cues exist (Willis, 2006).

To return to the Half Dome example, you would build memories based on the semantic content of the book you were reading. In addition, the exhilaration of the location would encode the information in episodic memory and tie it to the book in a completely different area of the brain. You could later recall what you read simply by thinking about Half Dome.

In previous generations, a common conversation topic was, "Where were you when you heard that John F. Kennedy was shot?" For those born in the second half of the 20th century, the question has now become, "Where were you when you heard about 9/11?" For me, I was in my classroom during my first year of teaching at Joy James Elementary in Fort Worth, TX. I distinctly remember my principal getting on the loudspeaker and announcing that something tragic had happened. That was it, nothing more. I quickly got online, though quick in 2001 is considered glacial today, and watched in horror as the reports filed in. My memories of that event are inextricably linked not only to the facts (semantic) but also the location (episodic).

In addition to the two types of explicit memories (i.e., semantic and episodic), there are many different classifications of implicit memories. These include procedural memories, priming memories, and conditioning memories such as reflexes, emotional intensity, and sensory information. Of these, one of the strongest links for memory retrieval is linking it to emotions (Jenson, 2005).

In the past, many thought that emotions and cognition comprised separate areas and functions within the brain. Modern neurological research techniques, however, have shown that the overlap between the two is so great that they can hardly be separated. It is very unlikely, in fact, for any learning to take place without emotions (Immordino-Yang & Damasio, 2007).

Emotions serve as memory anchors and also as a rudder for practical applications. When students access prior knowledge to evaluate and tackle new problems, neuroscience shows us that they do so within an emotional context. Emotions serve as a "rudder" to guide students on applying what they learn in social situations. Rather than being separate from rational thought, emotions are essential to memory creation and application (Immordino-Yang & Damasio, 2007).

Connecting new information with senses, activities, and emotions will help the brain more easily recall the information later. Instead of just reading about something, students should experience it and connect it to visual, auditory, tactile, and emotional areas of the brain. The more memory tags associated with the content, the more ways there will be to cue up the memory when needed (Willis, 2006).

Instructional Implications of Memory

Although this appendix lies within a book dedicated to vocabulary instruction, it could be transported to many other educational books with very little degradation of content. Since the aim of this book, along with all educational practices, is to influence the impact that learning has on students, a short review of mind and brain research seemed appropriate. What's the point of teaching something if students won't remember it even a week later?

The thought of a single lesson meeting the needs of a room full of students can be a bit daunting. With the vast majority of students preferring to learn visually and/or kinesthetically (Tate, 2016), simply talking to the students won't work. Verbal instruction alone will not only mesh with the preferred learning modality of just a small portion of the class, anything discussed will make few pathways into the brain.

Ideal lessons are those that stimulate various parts of the students' brains. They should participate in challenging and engaging tasks that stimulate multiple sensory systems. In striving to make sense of the experience, students should interact with the knowledge using a variety of methods. Their physical senses will be aroused, their emotions activated, and connections made to prior knowledge. The semantic, episodic, and emotional aspects of the activity should all work together to make the lesson one that will not be quickly forgotten (Willis, 2006).

A common conundrum asks the question, If a tree falls in the forest and no one is around to hear it, does it still make a sound? For the purposes of vocabulary instruction in particular and education in general, a better question exists. If students have been taught something but later can't recall it, did they ever really learn?

The teaching suggestions in this book are grounded in current knowledge of how our brains work. They are fun, engaging, and powerful. Below the surface, however, note that they are carefully designed multi-sensory experiences crafted to activate prior knowledge and maximize memory formation and retrieval.

Motivation

Another foundation of this book is student motivation. All of the instructional plans of teachers can be laid to waste by the simple disinterest of students. To make wise teaching decisions, educators should not only know how to best create memorable lessons but also what makes students tick. What motivates them to learn or not learn? How can teachers best engage students to increase attention and achievement? Educational research has detailed five facets of student motivation (Daffern, 2017/2018). Students are driven to engage or disengage in learning because of competence, relationships, autonomy, value, and emotions.

Competence

Sometimes students seek to learn something new simply to bolster their feelings of adequacy. They enjoy challenges and the thrill that comes from successfully completing them. On the other hand, feelings of low competence can bring learning to an abrupt halt. Most students will not take academic risks if they feel inadequate to the demands of the task.

Instructional techniques that build competence help motivate students and keep them engaged. Offering sufficient support during learning tasks will provide the security needed to try something new. Cultivating a growth mindset, as opposed to a fixed mindset, helps students realize that errors are a normal part of learning and it's what we do with those errors that makes us smarter.

Relationships

Most teachers intuitively understand the power of relationships in the classroom. Typically, they can point to a teacher they had that profoundly impacted their lives and served as an inspiration for their career choice. Teacher-student relationships, put simply, have the potential to radically alter the lives of students.

Beyond teacher relationships, however, larger social needs serve to motivate students. It might be working with a group, talking with a friend, or simply being a part of a positive climate that keep them engaged. Student interactions with peers and adults serve as a strong motivational factor for many students today.

Autonomy

In addition to competence and relationships, giving students a voice and a choice in learning can be immensely powerful. If you've ever been told, "You're not the boss of me," or been asked, "Do I have to?" you've seen autonomy at work. Human nature chafes at shackles and this tendency emerges at a very young age.

Teachers who are controlling usually see the opposite of what they hope to find. Instead of an orderly learning environment, dictatorial teaching styles typically inspire revolutionary tendencies in normally compliant students. When students have a sense of control and feelings of competence, intrinsic motivation begins to emerge.

Value

Learning that is not meaningful is ultimately forgettable. Like relationships, this facet of motivation is usually well understood by teachers. Real-world scenarios, problem-based learning, and even the relatively new idea of Genius Hour all serve to provide relevancy to student learning.

Tied to this idea of value is the goal orientation of students. When they participate in learning activities, what are their ultimate (and usually subconscious) goals? Are they learning to learn or learning to get a grade? Do they place greater value in knowledge or in accomplishments? The answers to these questions help shape the motivational facet of value.

Emotions

As previously mentioned, emotions are integral to learning as well as memory formation. In fact, there isn't much that happens that does not have an emotional tint. Emotions shape thinking, reasoning, judgment, and memory formation and retrieval.

Regarding motivation, emotions play a key part in triggering engagement or disengagement. When students are in a negative emotional state, all learning is halted and baser instincts take over. Emotions must be either neutral or positive before learning has a chance of sticking. One of the key emotions teachers should seek to trigger is interest.

Instructional Implications of Motivation

Engagement occurs when instructional design meets student motivation. With the five facets of motivation in mind, instruction should be designed to specifically target and harness student motivation. Why go through the trouble planning a lesson if it won't even keep the students' attention?

Though each facet of motivation was introduced separately, they actually intertwine and build on each other to create a student's motivational makeup. The instructional needs of student are not just one or two areas but a combination of all facets with relative peaks and valleys.

The teaching suggestions in this book are grounded in the truths of memory and motivation. Instruction that does not activate our brain's tendency for memory formation is not worth pursuing. Likewise, instruction that does not leverage student motivation will ultimately fall flat.

REFERENCES

Anderson, H. C. (1872). *Fairy Tales of Hans Christian Anderson.* (H. B. Paull, Trans.) Retrieved November 10, 2017, from http://hca.gilead.org.il/vt/

Anderson, R. C., & Nagy, W. E. (1993). The vocabulary conundrum. *Center for the Study of Reading Technical Report, no. 570.*

Beck, I. L., McKeown, M. G., Wagner, R. K., Muse, A. E., & Tannenbaum, K. R. (2007). Different ways for different goals, but keep your eye on the higher verbal goals. In *Vocabulary Acquisition: Implications for Reading Comprehension* (pp. 182-204).

Beck, I., & McKeown, M. (1991). Conditions of vocabulary acquisition. In R. Barr, M. L. Kamil, P. B. Mosenthal, & P. D. Pearson, *Handbook of Reading Research* (Vol. 2, pp. 789-814). Hillsdale, NJ: Lawrence Erlbaum Associates.

Blachowicz, C. L., & Fisher, P. (2004a). Keep the "Fun" in Fundamental. In J. F. Bauman, & E. J. Kame'enui (Eds.), *Vocabulary Instruction* (pp. 219-238). Guilford Publications.

Blachowicz, C. L., & Fisher, P. (2004b). Vocabulary lessons. *Educational Leadership, 61*(6), 66-69.

Blachowicz, C. L., Fisher, P. J., & Watts-Taffe, S. (2005). Integrated

Vocabulary Instruction: Meeting the Needs of Diverse Learners in Grades K-5. *Learning Point Associates/North Central Regional Educational Laboratory (NCREL)*.

Blachowicz, C. L., Fisher, P. J., Ogle, D., & Watts-Taffe, S. (2006). Vocabulary: Questions from the classroom. *Reading Research Quarterly, 41*(4), 524-539.

Blachowicz, C., & Fisher, P. (2011). A Word for the Words. *Educational Leadership, 68*(6).

Brief. (2008). *Effective Vocabulary Instruction, A Reading First Quality Brief.*

Carlisle, J. F. (2007). Fostering Morphological Processing, Vocabulary Development, and Reading Comprehension. In R. K. Wagner, A. E. Muse, & K. R. Tannenbaum (Eds.), *Vocabulary Acquisition: Implications for Reading Comprehension* (pp. 78-103). New York: The Guilford Press.

Daffern, A. (2017). *Solving Student Engagement: Designing Instruction to Motivate Every Student.* Aaron Daffern Consulting.

Daffern, A. (2018). *Don't Quit Your Day Job: An Educator's Guide to Student Engagement.* Aaron Daffern Consulting.

Echevarria, J., Frey, N., & Fisher, D. (2016). *How to Reach the Hard to Teach: Excellent Instruction for Those Who Need It Most.* Alexandria, VA: ASCD.

Fischer, K. W. (2009). Mind, brain, and education: building a scientific groundwork for learning and teaching. *Mind, Brain, and Education, 3*(1), 3-16.

Fisher, D., Frey, N., & Hattie, J. (2016). *Visible Learning for Literacy: Implementing the Practices That Work Best to Accelerate Student Learning.* Corwin Literacy.

Flanigan, K., & Greenwood, S. C. (2007). Effective content vocabulary instruction in the middle: Matching students, purposes, words, and strategies. *Journal of Adolescent & Adult Literacy, 51*(3), 226-238.

Glynn, S. M. (2007). The teaching-with-analogies model. *Science and Children, 44*(8), 52.

Glynn, S. M. (2008). Making science concepts meaningful to students: teaching with analogies. *Four Decades of Research in Science Education-From Curriculum Development to Quality Improvement*, 113.

Graves, M. F. (2015). Building a vocabulary program that really could make a significant contribution to students becoming college and career ready. In D. P. Pearson, & E. H. Hiebert (Eds.), *Research-Based Practices for Teaching Common Core Literacy.* Teachers College Press.

Graves, M. F. (2016). *The Vocabulary Book: Learning and Instruction.* Teachers College Press.

Graves, M. F., & Fitzgerald, J. (2006). Effective Vocabulary Instruction for English-Language Learners. In C. C. Block, & J. Mangieri (Eds.), *The vocabulary enriched classroom* (pp. 118-137). New York: Scholastic.

Graves, M. F., Baumann, J. F., & Blachowicz, C. L. (2014). Words, words, everywhere, but which ones do we teach? *The Reading Teacher, 67*(5), 333-346.

Immordino-Yang, M. H., & Damasio, A. (2007). We feel, therefore we learn: The relevance of affective and social neuroscience to education. *Mind, Brain, and Education, 1*(1), 3-10.

Jenson, E. (2005). *Teaching with the Brain in Mind.* ASCD.

Kelley, J. G., Lesaux, N. K., Kieffer, M. J., & Faller, S. E. (2010). Effective academic vocabulary instruction in the urban middle school. *The Reading Teacher, 64*(1), 5-14.

Marzano, R. J. (2009). The Art and Science of Teaching/ Six Steps to Better Vocabulary Instruction. *Educational Leadership, 67*(1), 83-84.

Marzano, R. J., & Pickering, D. J. (2005). *Building academic vocabulary: Teacher's manual.* Alexandria, VA: Association for Supervision and Curriculum Development.

Mebarki, Z. (2011). Vocabulary Knowledge and Reading Comprehension. *International Journal of Arabic-English Studies, 12*, 131-154.

Nagy, W. (2007). Metalinguistic Awareness and the Vocabulary-Comprehension Connection. In R. K. Wagner, A. Muse, & K. R. Tannenbaum (Eds.), *Vocabulary Acquisition: Implications for Reading Comprehension* (pp. 52-77). New York, NY: The Guilford Press.

Nagy, W. E. (1988). *Teaching Vocabulary To Improve Reading Comprehension.* Urbana, Ill.: ERIC Clearinghouse on Reading and Communication Skills.

Nagy, W. E., & Herman, P. A. (1984). *Limitations of vocabulary instruction.* Center for the Study of Reading Technical Report, no. 326.

Nagy, W., & Townsend, D. (2012). Words as tools: Learning academic vocabulary as language acquisition. *Reading Research Quarterly, 47*(1), 91-108.

Paris, N. A., & Glynn, S. M. (2004). Elaborate analogies in science text: Tools for enhancing preservice teachers' knowledge and attitudes. *Contemporary Educational Psychology, 29*(3), 230-247.

Phillips, D. C., Foote, C. J., & Harper, L. J. (2008). Strategies for effective vocabulary instruction. *Reading Improvement, 45*(2), 62.

Pressley, M., Disney, L., & Anderson, K. (2007). Landmark Vocabulary Instructional Research. In R. K. Wagner, A. E. Muse, & K. R. Tannenbaum (Eds.), *Vocabulary Acquisition: Implications for Reading Comprehension* (pp. 205-232). New York: The Guilford Press.

Pythian-Sence, C., & Wagner, R. K. (2007). Vocabulary acquisition: A primer. In *Vocabulary Acquisition: Implications for Reading Comprehension* (pp. 1-14).

Scott, J. A., & Nagy, W. E. (2009). Developing word consciousness. In M. Graves (Ed.), *Essential readings on vocabulary instruction* (pp. 106-117). Newark, DE: International Reading Association.

Silver, H. F., Strong, R. W., & Perini, M. J. (2007). *The strategic teacher: Selecting the right research-based strategy for every lesson.* ASCD.

Smith, C. B. (1997). *Vocabulary Instruction and Reading Comprehension. ERIC Digest.* Bloomington, IN: ERIC Clearinghouse on Reading English and Communication.

Stahl, S. A., & Fairbanks, M. M. (1986). The effects of vocabulary instruction: A model-based meta-analysis. *Review of Educational Research, 56*(1), 72-110.

Tate, M. L. (2016). *Worksheets Don't Grow Dendrites: 20 Instructional Strategies That Engage the Brain.* Corwin Press.

Willis, J. (2006). *Research-based Strategies to Ignite Student Learning.* Alexandria, VA: Association for Supervision and Curriculum Development.

About the Author

Aaron lives in Ft. Worth, TX, with his wife Heather, his children Dave, Drew, Desiree, and Daniel. He is an avid disc golfer and sports nut, closely following the Rangers, Cowboys, and Mavericks. He enjoys fantasy novels, Star Trek: The Next Generation, the Marvel Cinematic Universe, and reading peer-reviewed educational psychology research articles.

Before becoming an education consultant, Aaron spent 11 years in the classroom as a 3rd, 4th, and 6th grade teacher. He also spent several years as a campus and district administrator of a charter school in Arlington, TX.

If you would like to learn more about one- and two-day training options for schools and districts, visit him online at AaronDaffern.com. You can also email him at aarondaffern@gmail.com.

www.ingramcontent.com/pod-product-compliance
Lightning Source LLC
Chambersburg PA
CBHW071215160426
43196CB00012B/2314